THE INTERPRETERS

THE INTERPRETERS

BY

A. E.

"In Him we live and move and have our being."—St. Paul.
"What relation have the politics of time to the politics of
eternity?"—Leroy

"How can right find its appropriate might?"—Lavelle

CORACLE PRESS

San Rafael, Ca

Second, Facsimile edition,
Coracle Press, 2008
First edition, Macmillan and Co., 1922

For information, address:
Coracle Press, P.O. Box 151011
San Rafael, California 94915, USA

Library of Congress Cataloging-in-Publication Data

AE, 1867–1935.
The interpreters / by A. E. — 2nd facsimile ed.
p. cm.
ISBN 978-1-59731-316-2 (hardback: alk. paper)
ISBN 978-1-59731-315-5 (pbk.: alk. paper)
1. Religion and politics—Fiction. I. Title.

PR6035.U716 2008
823'.912—dc22   2008021909

TO

STEPHEN MACKENNA

FOR THE DELIGHT I HAVE

IN HIS NOBLE TRANSLATION OF PLOTINUS

PREFACE

I HAVE been intimate with some who risked
and with some who lost life for causes to
which they were devoted, and came to
understand that with many the political
images in imagination were but the psychic
body of spiritual ideas. Behind the open
argument lurked a spiritual mood which
was the true decider of destiny. Nations
conceive of themselves as guided or sustained
by a divine wisdom, and I have wondered
in what manner impulse might flow from
Heaven to Earth. Out of my meditation
on this came *The Interpreters.* Those who
take part in the symposium suppose of the
universe that it is a spiritual being, and
they inquire what relation the politics of
Time may have to the politics of Eternity.
Their varying faiths have been held by many
ancients and by some who are modern, but
the symposium has been laid in a future

century so that ideals over which there is
conflict to-day might be discussed divested
of passion and apart from transient circumstance. I was not interested in the creation
of characters but in tracking political moods
back to spiritual origins, and *The Interpreters* may be taken as a symposium between
scattered portions of one nature dramatically
sundered as the soul is in dream.

A. E.

I

On an evening in the late autumn a young
man was hurrying through the lit crowded
streets of his city, his mind but dimly aware
of his fellow-citizens, for he was raised above
himself by the adventure on which he was
bent, and what had been familiar seemed now
remote as the body is to the soul in spiritual
exaltation. Because the high purpose seeks
the companionship of high things, he paused
awhile, looking beyond the dark roofs,
where, over horizons of murky citron, the
air glowed through regions of passionate
green to a blue abyss becoming momentarily
more fathomless. Never to his eyes had
that vision appeared so beautiful, trembling
from one exquisite transience of colour to
another. Tall pillars crested with a ruby
glow marked the airways, and their dark
lines and lights sank westward over the
city. On each side the freighted galleons,
winged shapes of dusk and glitter, roared

overhead, whirring up swiftly from the
horizon or fading with all their glitter into
the green west. Not these hurrying lights
his eye sought, but those changeless lights
which have watched earth from its begin-
nings. Some cosmic emotion made him
feel akin with those heavenly lights. A
world empire was in trouble. A nation
long restless under its rule had resurrected
ancient hopes, and this young man with
many others was bent on a violent assertion
of its right to freedom. His imagination
had long passed beyond fear of death. But,
having in thought cast life aside, life strangely
had become richly augmented. He seemed
to himself a being of fire dwelling in a body
of air, so intense was feeling, so light his
limbs. In that mood the people in the
streets, on his own level yesterday, appeared
faint as shadows ; but as compensation a
new multitudinous life sprang up within him
as if all those who had his hope and were
with him in his deed had come to a mystic
unity in the spirit. In this dilation of consciousness he felt the gods were with him,
and it was then he looked up at the stars,
feeling in an instant of vision that he was
comrade with them and with all god-inspired

life, and they, with earth and its people, were sustained and directed by one inflexible cosmic will. He felt it strange he had not realised before how high was the enterprise to which he had been led by a study of the history and culture of his nation. He moved confidently as a warrior of antiquity with whom Athene or Hera went invisibly to battle. He was a poet, and because his soul was a treasure-house stored with the thoughts of the great who lived before him, he interpreted his own emotions as his more uneducated comrades never could have done, they whose action was instinctive, and whose minds were not subtle enough to discern the immortal mingling with their moods, and who would perhaps have lost enthusiasm if they had been told what purposes Nature had with them, and to what event, æons away, they were being led, and that this heroic enterprise of their life was but an hour's incident in a cyclic pilgrimage.

As he crossed an open square there came a roar which shook the air. An orange flame spurted athwart the dusky citron of the sky, and after that clouds of smoke, ruddily obscure, began to pile themselves up gigantically in the higher blue of night.

He gazed at this uprising of flame as the Israelites of old might have looked on the cloud and the fire which mantled the Shepherd of their host, for this was the signal that at the other end of the city the revolt had begun. Yet his body shivered, for the intelligence in it which stood sentinel guarding its mortality knew that this conflagration began a struggle in which itself might perish, and which for it would be the end of all. That mute appeal was unheeded, for the will of the young man was like a drawn bow, and life the arrow ready to be sped by the will. He experienced the terrible joy of life which has been emancipated. The spirit of man had risen from the grave which was fear, was emerging from that narrow prison cell like the sky-reaching genie from the little copper vessel in the tale of Arabian enchantment. Like a god it was laying hands on the powers of storm and commotion. Life had broken its moulds. It was no longer static but fluid, a river moving to some ocean. He watched the ruddily glowing smoke hungrily. Underneath it he imagined faces pale and bright. There were comrades, fearless, wilful, laughing, intoxicated as he was himself, breaking

the iron law of the Iron Age. After centuries of frustated effort the nation, long
dominated by an alien power which seemed
immutable, had a resurrection. It would
join the great procession of states, of beings
mightier than man created by man. It
would become like Egypt, Assyria, Greece,
or Rome. The genius of multitudes would
unite to give it spiritual greatness. Thoughts
like these thronged the brain of the young
man as he moved closer to the great building
which he and others had planned to take by
surprise. The moment arranged drew nigh.
Hundreds of men were mysteriously gathering, loitering with intent, gazing at the
distant illumination in the sky yet all the
time nearing the gate of the arsenal. What
had brought about that orchestration of life?
They were united in the deed. Were they
really united in soul? Was the same mood
in the heart of that sombre concentrated
workman as in the imaginative poet or that
sharp - featured cynical journalist? Were
they all raised above themselves by the same
aspiration? Here were men hardly able to
restrain themselves from action, which was
their life. Here were thinkers drawn by
some agony of conscience which bade them

leave the fireside and the intimate lives about it, trusting their young to a destiny which, had they thought over it, had ever seemed heedless of life. Had each one his own dream which he believed his nation would fulfil? Or was there a Wisdom moving all for purposes of its own? Was there an inexorable war waged by the gods upon humanity, shattering its peace, never allowing it to rest, shepherding the host from cycle to cycle until it had grown to power and those divine enemies became its kinsmen? Of what lay beneath that gathering the poet, for all his imagination, knew little, for he was so blinded by his own impulse that he imputed it to those who moved with him, that crowd which grew ever thicker, casting furtive glances at each other, at those they did not recognise, who might be agents of the power they sought to overthrow. Every heart heard its own beating. Here were resolute men who would act. Then the hour struck from a tall spire, bell after bell tolling slowly as if it symbolised the beating of the heart of the nation. On the instant men everywhere put on their sleeves the scarf which revealed all to each other. Those hitherto only known

to the leaders of their groups could now
recognise their comrades. Weapons of all
kinds were drawn forth. Voices rang out
sternly in command, and the crowd, a river
of fiery life, surged through the open gate
of the arsenal.

II

WE waken from dream, from a nightmare in which we fought with demons, to find the body cold, clammy, and trembling, but all recollection of that dark agony is soon lost beyond recall. The body still shudders but knows not why. Our ascents to Heaven, our descents into Hell, lay too high or too heavy a burden upon the soul for memory. It cannot mirror them for more than an instant, and they melt dreamlike from consciousness. Of the physical conflict in the arsenal the poet remembered little. It was blurred to his intellect by excess of energy or passion as objects are blurred to the eye by excess of light. He came back to himself at last crowded into a corner with a group of his surviving comrades, cut off from escape. Here at least the revolution had failed. Empires are like those beings in the Apocalypse full of eyes within and without. One of these eyes had discovered a detail of

the conspiracy and the open gate of the
arsenal was a trap. Another of these apoca-
lyptic eyes overlooked them searching for
persons of power among the rebels. They
were taken one by one as a finger pointed
them out. The poet was of these. He was
led by his guards up many steps and along
many dim-lit corridors and was halted at
last by a door about which armed men stood
sentinel. He was thrust within and the
door was locked behind him. He was
greeted by a tumult of gay and exalted
voices. It was a spiritual gaiety. The
voices had the exaltation of those who had
been engaged in a death struggle not so
much with others as with themselves and
had been conquerors. They could not have
explained why they were so gay. They were
prisoners and defeated. Some of them were
wounded. On the morrow they might be
standing with their backs to a wall taking
a wild farewell of the sky, drinking greedily
the last drop in the cup of life before a voice
called on the executioners to fire. The
exaltation was secret and of the spirit, for
all conflicts are at the last between soul and
body, and here the soul had triumphed ;
the immortal in each one had made a great

stride to conscious dwelling within them and it was sustaining them with its own lavish power. Outwardly they were but men who had not failed each other however they had failed in their enterprise. Their gaze on each other was frank and affectionate. The young poet was hailed uproariously by those who knew him. Others who had heard of him gazed on him with pride.

" All here for Valhalla ! "

" I also am a traveller," said the newcomer.

" They will never allow you to go, Lavelle. You might be admitted. There will be no lingering over our fate. Hell was built for such rascals as we are."

" Hush, fools, we may be out before day-break. Does that sound like a city subdued ? "

The room was reddening in a glow from without. There was a rattle increasing in intensity, not in one place but over the city. Then came a sinister noise like a sabre of sound swishing through the air, and deeper and more tremendous notes boomed from further distances.

" See ! see ! " cried one. " The air lights have gone out."

They crowded to the windows. The towering poles which had lifted up their

red lamps through the dusk to guide the
night journeying airships were now lightless
and darkly silhouetted against glowing masses
of smoke. The airships were scattering,
flying wildly, like winged dragons on some
fabulous adventure who had met a volcano
in eruption on their path. Some had
ascended, their lights scintillating remotely
in the higher darkness, while others in lower
levels flashed flame-coloured against the blue,
their wings gilded with fire from the glowing
city below.

" They must come down !   They will be
ours !   There were men ready to rush the
boats. They cannot risk passage east or
west with the ways unlighted ! "

Rumour started mysteriously among the
prisoners. Some one had heard or surmised
something, and in the fever of feeling it
grew in a moment, like a phantasmal tree
created by the magic of a faquir, to be of
gigantic import. This rumour dwindled to
give place to others more exciting. The
poet soon turned away, gazing through a
window at the spectacle of the night which
never tired him. Imagination was at work.
It created huge figures of gods seated on
the mountains that lay around the city,

figures still as if cast in gold, with immense
pondering brows bent downward, waiting,
perhaps, for god folk to rise up from men
folk out of that furnace into which so many
had cast themselves as a sacrifice.

" You should feel proud as Helen looking
over the ruins of Troy."

An intense guttural voice was in his ear.
Lavelle turned round and saw a pallid face
with beaked nose, lips thick but not sen-
sual, humorous rather, even mocking, quick-
moving black eyes like polished ebony, bushy
grey brows and hair, every feature carved and
etched by mind, the head large on a shrunken
body.   It was the writer he had seen in the
crowd, Leroy, a notoriety, in whose work
fantastical humour hardly disguised the
agony of the idealist without faith in society.
There existed between himself and the poet
that attraction which opposites have for each
other.   His feeling for Lavelle was friendly,
almost tender.   He looked sorrowfully upon
the face of the young poet so unlike his own,
upon a noble beauty whose invisible sculptors
were ecstasy, ardour, and the music of
murmured or chanted speech.

" Why ? "

" Why, who created the spirit of this

revolt ? Who led the people to quit the
beer which gives peace, to drink the heady
wine of imagination ? Who ransacked the
past and revived the traditions of the nation ?
Who but you found in the fairy tales of its
infancy the basis of a future civilisation ?
The wine has gone to peoples' heads.
What are they doing ? Thinking they are
building a heaven on earth while they are
fighting like devils ! "

"Ah !" said the poet. " I wish it were
true. But you know how little high traditions move the people."

" It may be so with them but not with
the leaders. The people may not guess the
thoughts that move the mightier of their
kind but they follow all the same. And the
leaders are aglow from a phosphorescence
engendered in the brains of poets like you,
or imaginative historians like Brehon. What
is it they are led by in the end but a fragile
thought ; a coloured dream ; a thing of
air ! "

" No ! no !" said Lavelle impetuously.
" It is not unreal. Heaven is in the kindled
spirit of man. How do you come to be
here yourself ? Are you not with us ? For
what but a dream do you cast away life ? "

" Oh," said the other, " I am an anarchist and I wish to be free, and also my Dark Angel told me there was nothing real in my character and I wished to test it."

" What did you find in yourself ? "

" Nothing ! More foam on wilder waters ! But who is this ? "

The door had opened again, and a man, by attire, manner, and voice evidently a personage, was pushed in backwards protesting vehemently of his innocence, that he was not a rebel, that he hated them, when an ungentle thrust from the weapon of his guard cut short speech from him, and he was propelled from the doorway into the room.

" You can explain all that to-morrow," said a surly voice, evidently sceptical that the prisoner could explain the circumstance which caused his arrest. The door was again closed. The newcomer turned to face the curious and not too friendly faces of the prisoners.

" You are the fanatics who have upset the city ! I hope there will not be one of you alive to-morrow night ! "

" Sir," said Leroy. " I do not know how you came to be here, but I am sure it is not your good angel who inspires you to speak as you do. There are some here who might insist on your escape through the window, and the distance from the window to the pavement is exactly the distance from life to death."

" I think I know who this is," said another prisoner. Then turning to the last arrival he asked, " Why did they take you ? You are not of us."

The newcomer was quieting, his agitation overcome by the coolness of those about him. He had picked up a coloured scarf in the street, missing the owner who was hurrying on, and he was still holding it when he was arrested by a patrol. The scarf was worn by those active in the revolt. One of the prisoners whispered to Leroy it was more likely the arrest was made because of the prisoner's personal likeness to one of their own leaders. The newcomer mentioned his name, Heyt, the autocrat of one of those great economic federations which dominated state policy and whose operations had created deep bitterness among the revolting people. The name was greeted with roars of laughter. The patrol had arrested a pillar of state.

" The guilty on both sides in the same prison ! " cried Leroy. " I never believed

Deity had any attributes but I must now endow it with the attribute of humour. Sir," he said, turning to Heyt. " If you should be shot before me to-morrow you may die with the consolation that your death has shaken a sceptic in his unbelief."

Heyt, whose features had assumed the expression of haughtiness which seemed habitual to them, looked disdainfully at Leroy and made no reply. He sat down on a bench which ran along by the wall, ignoring his fellow-prisoners, who also ignored him as an unlikely source of information about the progress of the revolt. The excitement began to dwindle, a more solemn mood to replace the gaiety and to turn their thoughts to that other world, in which, had they known it, they already existed, entering it in all hours of intense and deeper being. Even to the heaven-lit spirit of the saint the prospect of death and the transit from familiar things induces solemnity of feeling, though the heart has the certitude that there is the heart's desire. These for the most part had taken little thought of that morrow or what spiritual raiment might be put on them, but they remembered the popular persistent talk about death and judgement, and they began to speculate among themselves upon such things as men who knew their stay here may be short and who must think of their further travelling. Leroy with his back to them listened irritably to their anticipations of death and after. Looking out through a window he began whistling softly and savagely to himself. That men who were in revolt against the conventions of this world should accept the conventions of the next world, which to him were even more objectionable, angered him so that he could hardly trust himself to speech.

III

It is rarely that a single mood stays long with those who believe they are nigh to death. A horde of thoughts and feelings rush from the subconscious as if they knew how little time remained for them to prove themselves. There is swift reaction. Leroy's desperate mood soon passed, his ironic humour kindled by the desire of a prisoner for consolation by a priest of his church.

" Do you really believe his blessing will secure you welcome in the Kingdom of Heaven ? " he said. "My Dark Angel tells me there has been very little difference between his ideas of religion and the churches' for a very long time, so little, indeed, that his master was thinking of quietly dropping his old title and calling himself God. Myself I hold the substitution was effected centuries ago and was quite unnoticed. Everything went on as before. The princes of religion sat undisturbed upon episcopal thrones. I think," he added grimly, "their long and faithful services to their new master merit sympathetic consideration from the Judge of all the world."

The prisoners gathered laughing around Leroy. His resolute spirit dominated the rest as resolute spirits do all men in time of peril. They began to even their mood to his.

" Come, tell us all about it ! What is to be our fate ? Will there be another court-martial in Heaven when we are despatched here ? "

" What are we guilty of before Heaven ? What relation have the politics of time to the politics of eternity ? Are we concerned with the battles of beasts in the jungle, or the pursuit and flight under the waters ? If there are beings above us, not of our order, how do we offend them ? Do we throw Heaven into disorder when we revolt against tyranny here ? I do not think the ridge-pole of the universe is so fragile as to be shaken by our rubbing ourselves against it."

" I think," said Lavelle, " that Heaven and Earth must be a unity, and that men are often Heaven inspired, and that ideas descend on us from a divine world, and they must finally make a conquest of Earth and draw us into a conscious unity with the Heavens. If the universe is a spiritual being, everything finally must be in harmony with it, and wild creatures, the elements even, undergo a transfiguration, fierce things becoming gentle, and——"

" The shark becoming vegetarian," interrupted Leroy. " O Lavelle, Lavelle, you are the imperialist of idealism. When you had remade the nation in your own image you would impose the law of your being upon the world. Even the fishes would be swept into your net. How wise was the Chinese sage who said ' when a man begins to reform the world I perceive there will be no end to it.' There would be no place in your universe for an individualist like myself. I would be a gnat irritating its spiritual body."

" You may laugh at the marriage of Heaven and Earth," Lavelle spoke again. " But there is a power behind ideas. I remember what a dispirited group met to discuss the revolt, what a burden lay upon every heart. Yet when we decided to act for the nation what a magical transformation took place ! How joyful every one became !

They were gay and laughed and cried as
if it was resurrection morn. What was the
source of that joy ? By what alchemy was
the chill made fiery ? I felt glowing as if
Heaven had lifted me up to itself. What
was that but the power of an idea ? You
felt it yourself. Is there one even here who
would wish now to withdraw ? Would we
not all prefer death with our nation fighting
against the rule of the iron powers ? "

" No, no, not one of us repents," cried
the prisoners.

" I prefer to be here, it is true," said
Leroy. " But I cannot convince myself that
I am not a fool. It is ludicrous to me to
feel heroic irrational emotions welling up in
me overturning reason. It is doubtless
heredity. Some remote ancestor of mine
ought to be executed in my place."

" No, no, Leroy. The heroic is the deep
reality in you and all of us. It is translucent
to spirit and the will of Heaven is seen in
its actions."

" Are our actions then all Heaven inspired?
If I am anything I am an anarchist. I would
break up tyrannies because I am a lover of
liberty. I wish to be free to come and go,
to do or not to do, to think as I will, to speak

as I will. You would have your nation free
that it might come under another domination,
that there might be but one cultural mood
in it. You want an orchestration of life so
that every one in the nation may have the
same character and their works make one
harmony. There is Rian, who is an artist.
I think he is with us truly because the state
does not create beauty. I found him in a
rage cursing the last imperial edifice in our
city. It was designed by a blockhead, he
said, to house blockheads whose work it
would be to make the whole nation into
blockheads. Men ought to revolt against
a state which imposes a dull ugliness upon
us all our lives. Was not that so, Rian ? "
Leroy said to a young man who was listening
to the talk.

" Well, it helped to bring me here any-
how," said Rian, smiling.

" Rian is fighting for beauty. Between
himself and Heaven that is his motive. He
is a creature of æsthetic passions. Put
power into his hands and he would arrest
people for wearing inharmonious colours in
the streets. Our great Culain is a socialist.
He has an economic ideal while you have a
cultural ideal. I think every one who is

with us turned different faces to Heaven in
their prayers. Does Heaven accept them
all ? Are all these conflicting ideals in the
cosmic plan ? If it approves everything it
designs nothing. I am sure too that there
are those fighting against us who believe
their empire is a manifestation of the Absolute, and they are filled with as pure a
glow as you are."

" Do you really believe, Leroy, that the
same quality of inspiration can exist in
opposites ? "

" Well, the opposites at least are willing
to pay for their inspiration in the same coin of
life as you are. Is it not better to base your
case simply on obvious right than to bring
in a mystical theory of nationality. Every
people to-day fights in the name of God. The
ancients were more logical. They had tribal
deities. But you, my dear Lavelle, while
you are satisfied with your tribe on earth, claim
that all Heaven is with you. In one of the
old tales of our people it is told of two heroes
that they paused and embraced in the midst
of their conflict. They saw noble things in
each other. Life was a game to be played
nobly as indeed you play it ; but if you insist
on Heaven as the ally of your race you can

only suppose that the forces of Hell are behind your antagonist, and then there is an end of chivalry. You cannot weep over the fallen. You can only curse them as that old savage Dante denied pity to the spirit that uprose out of the miry pool in the Inferno."

" But you have too subtle a mind to believe the soul of man is completely isolated, is a being by itself and receives no light except from the sun, stars, and lamp-posts."

" We exist, it is true, in some miraculous being which bathes us, but I do not know whether it does not lend itself to my whimsies, whether it is not a mirror of our being rather than we of it. When I dream I create like a God, but I know my dreams spring out of my desires. Though they seem to melt into infinity I know that infinity is an illusion in the hollow of my brain. I dreamed a few nights ago that I saw God, really an august being, moving on His rolling throne through His dominions contemplating His children the stars. He came close to our earth, but had to skip back very quickly, so high up were the shells bursting, and the anti-aircraft guns were taking no chances with suspicious lumin-

osities.   He called me and asked ' What is
the trouble here ? ' and I said, ' Lord, it is
a spiritual conflict.'   ' That interests me.
Tell me all about it.'   And I explained that
the people of the earth were at war to decide
whether they would receive their culture
from such organs of public opinion as ' The
Horn of Empire ' or ' The Clarion of the
People,' and old God looked at me and looked
through me, and He burst out laughing, and
He laughed and laughed until the æther began
rocking, and on the waves of the æther the
stars went dancing and scintillating, tossing
up and down in the wildest gymnastics, like
corks on wild waters.   I pretended to be
amused also, but I really could not see what
the joke was about.   Then I awoke hearing
people laughing uncontrollably below my
window, and it was that laughter caused the
dream.   It was a miraculous creation in a
second, but I know it sprang out of my
humour.   You, if you dreamed, would see
a vision so beautiful that you would imagine
it was a vision of Paradise, but it would be
no less of yourself than my fantasy.   That
magical element which bathes us would have
made itself for you a mirror with the illusion
of infinite reality, just as it made itself a

theatre and supplied the properties to stage my ironic imagination. Perhaps that miraculous element which creates illusions in us with such swiftness may be God, and It may like a joke about Itself. Now neither you nor Rian would admit my fantasy was a divine revelation, though it was swift, coherent, and complete, in fact as much a miracle as any vision of Ezekiel."

" I'll admit it. There is character and originality in it," said the artist.

" I would not despair, if I had time, of proving your imagination an extension of the imagination of our ancestors," laughed Lavelle.

Leroy placed his hand affectionately on the shoulder of the poet. He was an older man than any there, more master of himself, and he was talking deliberately to lead a reaction of mood to the normal after the fierce excitement of the struggle in which they had been captured. Leroy and Lavelle were men who lived by intellect and imagination, and to the last their outlook would be intellectual rather than bodily ; but there were some of the prisoners who were realists and who had no interest in metaphysical discussion, and these had been watching with passionate interest everything in the city which could be seen from the high windows from which they gazed. There came a shout from these, and all hurried to the windows of the great room to see what new action was taking place in the drama in whose yet unfolded finale their fate was hidden.

IV

LAVELLE gazing from the high window saw
at first only the restless and ruddy glimmering of fire and shadow over the city.
But looking up he saw the vision which had
excited his companions. The guardians of
empire had sent a summons for aircraft to
overawe the revolting people, and they were
coming, a blazing caravan travelling across
the limitless desert of the sky. Not Babylon
nor Luxor to overawe the denizens of their
cities ever created in the squat magnificence
of their palaces such images of power as
these dragons of the air which drew up from
far horizons. Irresistible and disdainful as
eagles of a tumult of earth-crawling mice,
they floated with all their lights displayed
that the city might know what might overhung it. The air everywhere was vibrant
from the deep purring of their engines, and
it shook as Heaven might have shaken at
the opening of the seals in the Apocalypse.

The heart felt strained dreading, not individual doom, but the annihilation of cities
and races. The conflict below was now too
interknit for action, but the ships floated
high up like palaces of gods built on some
mountain slope of night, minatory to those
who gazed and who knew not at what instant
the glow of life might be extinguished in an
obliterating rain from the sky. From these
aerial cruisers the high admirals of empire
overawed the subject peoples. There was
nothing which could oppose them in the
underworld. Their crews were apart from
the earth-dwelling races, made distinct by
the ecstasy of the high air they breathed, by
a culture and poetry of their own fully intelligible only to the air-dwellers. Lifted
up by pride and united by a spirit which
seemed almost a new manifestation of cosmic
consciousness, they regarded themselves less
as servants of the empire than as acting
under a mandate from Heaven to keep the
peace of the world. Their vision of earth
was wide and etherealised, for there were no
frontiers to the realm they travelled in. Their
isolation begot dreams disdainful of the differences between races. A world empire was
the only politic which harmonised with their

mood, and they were ruthless in suppression
of revolt in territories whose people remembered an ancient sovereignty over themselves.
Nothing exasperates the spirit in man more
than power which seems unconquerable and
which makes impotent all protest. One of
the prisoners cursed bitterly. But with
Lavelle, the poet in him made him for an
instant almost traitor to his nation, stirred
as he was by that vision of the culmination of
human power soaring above the planet. The
problem of the interpretation of cosmic consciousness raised by Leroy recurred to him.
Was his sense of an infinity in his emotion
a criterion of truth, or was that antiquity
true that might indicated right? Did the
long overflow of power through centuries
into the organism of empire reveal a harmony
with cosmic purpose? Or was that vast
being in which all life germinated as in-
different to the creatures which became in
it as the night which enveloped the passionate
city in an even calm? The thinkers of his
time had divined an all-pervading element
by which life seemed to be manifested. By
it everything was born. Thought and desire
by it were translated into deed and energy.
It lay between the seed and the corn, between

the germ and the fulfilled being.   It seemed
to vitalise the good and the bad indifferently.
As a child equally pleased by flower or
glittering serpent, so this omnipotent child
seemed to delight equally in bringing to
birth monstrous and beautiful forms in
nature.   That miraculous element withheld
itself from nothing which desired manifestation in nature or man.   To some, like the
poet, it gave the vision of beauty, and to
others, to those who floated so high in the
æther, it gave almost an omnipotence of
power.   He felt how frail were his dreams
for such a battle as he was engaged in ; as
frail as clouds cast aside like smoke from
the prow of an aerial cruiser.   Turning away
with bitterness in his heart he was aware of
Leroy by his side.

" Leroy," he said, " I understand the
stories of men who sold themselves to a
devil.   There are powers which seem as if
they would be overcome only by supernatural power.   What forces can we summon
up to deliver us from these ? "

" Well, by our death we may become
supernatural beings ourselves, and so assail
our conquerors with legions of spirits.   The
primitive believed he absorbed the spirit of

the savage he killed and added its force to
his own, which perhaps meant that he felt
the foe within himself fighting beyond
death. Most of our comrades are quite
savage enough to continue fighting in that
way."

" Leroy, I can find no comfort in fantasies.
Can you, in the evolution of world forces,
foresee what may bring about the downfall
of power such as we see yonder in the sky?
We could not submit to it. We took the
only way we knew. We die and go out.
Yet I feel there must be a way even in this
world by which right may find its appropriate might. If there be no way we
are only struggling against the nature of
things."

" I think a revolt so widespread in the
world must shake them even up yonder in
their heaven, and I do not believe the influence of the dead on the living is altogether
a fantasy. The victors in great wars have
always been spiritually defeated by the
conquered. Rome came to be dominated
by Greek culture, and in the world war some
centuries ago the last vengeance of the dying
German Empire on its conquerors was to
imprint on them its own characteristics.

Your poetry and Brehon's History will be favourite studies in imperial circles in a few years."

The poet smiled but faintly. He was one of those who suffer on behalf of their nation that agony which others feel over personal misfortunes. He pursued his meditation dreamily. Why did the Earth spirit inspire so many millions of its children in such contrary ways? Could a cosmic plan be divined amid these opposites? Had Earth any dream of a culmination of her humanity, or was there some trouble in the heavenly house, a division of purpose among gods? He might himself soon be absorbed into that being, and in the light of that new dawn of consciousness his thoughts were less about his own race and its immediate problems than about ultimates. He might have pursued this obscure meditation further, only the door opened, and two figures appeared in the doorway, their faces dark and undistinguishable against the light beyond. They were thrust in by the guards and the door again closed. Out of the shadow one of the newcomers, a huge figure of a man, came forward. The red light through a window fell upon him and a cry of dismay broke from the prisoners. "Oh, it is Culain! Culain!" and they crowded about the man by whose influence the workers of the nation had been brought to take part in the revolt.

V

THE figure which emerged from the shadowy into the red air was massive, noble, and simple. It might have stood for an adept of labour or avatar of the Earth spirit incarnated in some grand labourer to inspire the workers by a new imagination of society. To the workers this Culain appeared an almost superhuman type of themselves, a clear utterer of what in them was inarticulate. That deep, slow, thrilling voice myriads had listened to as the voice of their own souls. It affected Lavelle strangely as it came, the one thing firm and tranquil, out of the excited mass of prisoners. Every figure in that group was momentarily changing in a moth-like flickering from pale to dark caused by the leaping of flame or rolling of smoky clouds over the city. Everything appeared unreal, the room itself, face, limb, body, mass, all that the imagination normally rested upon as solid seemed vague and thin as

35

dream. Only that deep voice seemed real
as if it was the undisturbed voice of immortality.

"No! No!" that deep voice was saying.
"It is not over. It is only beginning.
It is an earth movement. All that will
topple from the sky before it is over." And
he waved a hand towards the glittering
menace in the air.

"But we have no sky craft of our own!"

"If the roots deny sap the leaves fall from
the tree. They have the air now but we
have the earth. We are not using violence.
We deny labour. Every tributary which
fed them with power ceases to flow from
to-day. For a while they may rain death,
but they must descend and be as we are."

"I wish I could believe that," cried one.
"But their power comes from sources beyond
our control."

"This is not a revolt of two or three
nations. It is a revolt of humanity. To
you it may be a rebellion of your nation.
To us it is a revolution. The workers of
the world have dreamed towards this for
centuries. They are organised and know
now their own power and their own hearts.
They wish nations to be free, but they wish

more to be free themselves. We would not be in this struggle merely to exchange world masters for nation masters. The workers will have no master except their own collective will. All who have tried to raise humanity from above have only pressed more weightily on those below. Those who are beneath life alone can raise life. To-morrow no ships will leave harbour. No waggons will carry on land. The air will soon be empty. The armies will starve if they fight. Our terms of peace are the surrender of the world to the workers of the world."

Here indeed was vaster trouble than the prisoners had planned, or imagined possible, though they might have known that never did one wild power awaken in the world but its kinsmen followed fast as the wild riders follow one another in the vision of St. John.

" It is a new tyranny," muttered Leroy.

" I am with it," cried Rian the artist. " We will make something out of this old world after all. Culain, I will design the most wonderful cities for you if we ever get out of this. We will build palaces for everybody. I have always hated designing houses for the rich. It seemed like the sin of simony, selling beautiful imaginations for

money.   We artists built first for the gods
and we did our best work for them.   Since
then we have built for the Caesars, the
aristocracies, and the oligarchies, and our
work was worse with every change of
masters.   To work for the world will be
like working for the gods again."

"The more masters you have the worse
will it be," growled Leroy.

"Cannot you see the majestic things harmony of effort makes possible, old grumbler
that you are?" said Rian.   "I have looked
at the remains of the Parthenon, and have
sat for days brooding over the ruins of
temples in Egypt.   The people who saw
such beauty and magnificence must have
been proud and uplifted in heart.   However
mean their original nature they lived in an
atmosphere of greatness.   That divine architecture must have coloured their thought as
a sunset makes everything in harmony with
its own light.   If the empire had created
beauty I might have been with it.   I am
afraid I could always be bribed by fairy gold.
But it cannot create.   It can only suppress.
It multiplies images of stupidity everywhere.
Beauty is flying from the grey cities and the
mean streets where people live out their

lives. If this continues, humanity will grow
grey and ugly as the world it lives in. We
will forget what beauty means. It will be
a word with lost meanings like the Etruscan
inscriptions. You are frightened at the idea
of any kind of state as a mouse is of a trap.
Such oppression as we live under I will
revolt against with you. But I have imagination of a state of another character. You
are so much an individualist that you speak
as if every man was a distinct species of
being by himself, that no harmonious action
was possible, and we were all as apart in
character from each other as the lion is from
the tiger."

" We are really much more distinct from
each other than animals of different species
are," Leroy retorted. " One law for the
lion and the tiger would not be oppression.
They have the same appetites. The lion
and the tiger go one path to the pool to
drink and to the same covert to stalk the
same prey. Our souls drink from a pool
deeper and wider than ocean. You and I
see different eternities. We have the universe to roam in in imagination. It is our
virtue to be infinitely varied. The worst
tyranny is uniformity."

" Do you conceive of that being within you as indefinite in character and purpose ? " a quiet voice behind Leroy made question. Lavelle, Rian, and Leroy turned. They saw a tall, slightly stooping man, white-haired, a face aquiline and eager, the dark eyes with fire in them which turned from one to another indicating unabated intellectual vigour. It was the prisoner who had entered behind Culain, but who had been overlooked in the excitement caused by the entrance of so notable a personality. The name of the newcomer was familiar to all, but Lavelle alone recognised the historian of the nation. " How do you come to be here, sir ? " he asked. " You were not in our councils, though you are the father of us all."

" Well, since you young men made a bible of my history, our rulers seem to think it is better I should be out of the way while the trouble you created continues."

" People think the state obtains information by incredibly secret methods," said Leroy. " I believe it occupies itself in an incredibly unintelligent study of popular journals. It is sufficient for it to find a name there associated with a thing to

warrant arrest. But after all it only antici-
pates. If its prisoners are not guilty before
arrest they are ready to join any conspiracy
afterwards."

"I shall not regret my loss of liberty,"
said the newcomer. "I am sure I would
hear nothing so interesting without these
walls as I shall hear within them."

Fifty years before, when national sentiment
appeared almost extinct, Brehon, then a
young man, proposed to himself to write
the history of his country, and in the labour of
twenty years he had unveiled so extraordinary
a past, so rich a literature, in a language
almost forgotten, that his work became an
object of passionate study by his countrymen,
and what had been intended almost as a
funeral oration or panegyric over a dead
nation had the effect of rekindling it, and
it came forth young and living from its
grave. The historian had been followed by
creative writers like Lavelle, in whom the
submerged river of nationality again welled
up shining and life-giving. The youth of
the nation bathed in it, washing from their
souls the grime of empire, its mechanical
ideals, and the characterless culture it had
imposed on them. But after his history

had appeared, the historian seemed to take
no interest in the great movement he had
inspired. He became absorbed in more
abstruse studies, the nature of which was
known to but few among his countrymen.

"I have for a long time thought revolu-
tions spring from other than the ostensible
causes to which they are attributed, though
these may seem adequate. Even in the
moments I have been here I have heard
reference to principles which are not com-
monly discussed. You," said the historian,
addressing Leroy, " were explaining some
political ideal as being an extension of a
spiritual concept."

"Oh, if the people fighting without there
had only known the ideas Lavelle and Leroy
discuss among themselves, there would have
been no revolt," said Rian. "They would
not have understood what their leaders were
talking about. The room before you came
in was less like a prison for rebels than an
academy of philosophers discussing what
relation the politics of time had to the politics
of eternity."

"Could we not continue that discussion
and try to discover whether political emotions
are not in reality spiritual emotions?" asked

the historian. " The poets and lovers before
Plato traced the divine ancestry of love,
and other emotions have been related by the
mystics to divine originals. Yet political
emotions, which are as profound as any,
and are powerful enough to draw the lover
away from love, are not made sacred by
association with an Oversoul. Historical
and objective origins are attributed to passions
deep and absorbing as those evoked by great
religions. We shall not sleep here to-night,
I fancy ; and how could we employ the
hours better than by each telling as between
himself and Heaven what imagination about
society brought him to consider his imagination more important than life."

" As between myself and Heaven," said
Rian, " I believe I desired passionately to
build the palaces and cities of dream here
on the earth, and I wanted the prophets of
beauty like Lavelle to prepare the way in
people's souls. I never peered inside myself
except to search for unearthly compounds
of stone and mortar. But Lavelle and
Leroy have probed deeper things in their
being. Lavelle will tell us what brought
him from dream to action. We cannot
spend the night better. Tell us, Lavelle,

how the national idea turned a poet into a fighter. You were moved, I know, by impulses you never uttered to the crowds you inspired. I suspect you talked, like Moses, to gods upon the mountains."

VI

" Where else," answered Lavelle, " but on
lone earth or mountain come inspiration,
and how but by divine visitations, whisper-
ings and breathings from the dark were
nations inspired ? Every race, Greek,
Egyptian, Hindu, or Judaean, whose culture
moves us deeply, looked back to divine
origins. My belief in such inspirations has,
I confess, been more to me than the thoughts
about the nation I have shared with others.
But I do not know if I can make clear
reasons for my belief in an oversoul guiding
and inspiring our people. You will agree,
I think, that we do not bring about revolu-
tions because of the few people we may
know personally. We do so because of the
millions we do not know. And I think it is
true also that we are stirred less by the ideas
we make clear to ourselves than by the
myriad uncomprehended ideas and forces
which pour on us and through us, which

are hardly intelligible to ourselves, which we cannot rationalise, but which give us impulse, direction, and the sensation of fulness of being."

" I guess what you mean," said Rian. " I rarely designed a building without imagination creating a city in harmony with it ; and from this piling up of fanciful cities in the imagination comes the inspiration for the single house."

" Do you see the buildings in your imaginary city clearly ? " asked Lavelle.

" I do in part. Sometimes I can see the sun shining on architrave, carving, or pillar, casting clear-cut shadows. This I think strange and wonder how it all was born in me. I often feel a mere craftsman employed by a supernatural architect to carry out a few of his prodigal designs."

" You believe," Brehon asked of Lavelle, " these intuitions about the nation have their origin in a being which has an organic life of its own, just as the half-perceived buildings of imagination with him give the sense they are really complete like a city in the heavens before he becomes aware of them ? "

" Yes, I think that is a parallel. But Rian, for all his vision of cities, would find it difficult to draw in detail one after another the buildings he surmises in that architectural atmosphere around the one building he concentrates on. It is no less difficult for me to give substance to a multitude of feelings, which, if I pass them through a filter of words, will not sound like planetary murmurs, though I feel they come out of the soul of the world. I will try, however, to isolate some of these moods and interpret them. I feel it is easier now to do this because here we are, it may be, in the antechamber of death where unrealities are rare visitors. Here I find the thoughts I shared with others fade in power and the spiritual concept of nationality alone remains with me."

" I think we shall have some light on the problem how theocratic states were born," said Leroy. " Lavelle is an antique."

" It is a long history, beginning when I was a boy," said the poet, who accepted the ironical comment of his friend with good nature. " You remember, Rian, our holiday among the mountains ? One day you wished to climb to the top of the hill, and I would not, and you went on, and for hours I was alone. But as I lay on the hillside I was no longer solitary, but smitten through and through with another being, and I knew it was the earth, and it was living, and its life was mingling with my own. Some majesty was shining on me all the day, nodding at me behind the veil of light and air, or playing hide-and-seek within the shade, or it was in me as a spirit beseeching love from my own. It seemed older than life, yet younger and nigher to me than my own boyhood. I lay there drenched in the light, and all the while imagination, as a cloud which wanders between the Earth and Heaven, was wandering between my transience and some immortal youth. I can remember that magical day. I can see the white sun blinding the sky, and light in dazzling cataracts outpoured and foam from cloud to cloud, and the earth glow beneath an ocean of light with purple shaded valleys, and lakes that mirrored back the burning air, and woods vaporous as clouds along the hills, and jutting crags, and mountains hewn in pearl, all lustrous as dream images and all remote as dream. Earth had suffused its body with its soul, and I lay on the mountain side clinging to it in a passion. When Rian came down I heard his voice beside me as from an immense distance calling me back to myself ; and I was irritated by his coming, for I wanted to be alone with that spirit which had found me."

" Oh, I know," groaned Leroy. " If nature catches the soul young it is lost to humanity."

" No, no, the Earth spirit does not draw us aside from life. How could that which is father and mother of us all lead us to err from the law of our being ? "

" The earth may be our mother," retorted Leroy, " but I am sure it is not our father. We get intellect from something beyond planets or sun."

" Be quiet, Leroy," said Rian, " we will hear your reasons for revolution later. I am sure they will be the maddest of all, though Lavelle's political thinking appears to me to begin in very abstract regions."

" No, there are the true realities," cried the poet. " Abstractions begin when we get away from the Earth spirit which has begotten us. Out of it have come plant, animal and man—all real things. Do plant and animal arrange their own evolution ? Does the flower dream its own colour and scent ? Does the bee devise its own wings or the polity of the hive ? Are we less

E

exempt from that dominion over our ways ? Since I was born some wisdom, never sleeping though I slept, was in me, and cell by cell I was fashioned and woven together and over my making I had no control. We dwell in the house of the body, but its perfection and intricate life are the work of a wisdom which never relaxes dominion over a single cell. I believe that wisdom is within the soul to guide it. It is ready at every instant to declare to us the evolutionary purpose. It has planned for us a polity as it has planned for the bee the polity of the hive. We are higher than plant or animal. We can be conscious co-workers with the spirit of nature. We fall into unreal fantasy or thin abstraction when we think apart from it. We are empty as a vessel turned downward which fills itself only with air. If we think with the Earth spirit our souls become populous with beauty, for we turn the cup of our being to a spring which is always gushing."

" The Earth spirit speaks with one voice to you on your mountain and with another voice to some solitary in a desert in Araby."

" The Earth spirit throws itself into innumerable forms of life," answered Lavelle.

"Did you expect it to make its children all of one pattern? For every race its own culture. Every great civilisation, I think, had a deity behind it, or a divine shepherd who guided it on some plan in the cosmic imagination. 'Behold,' said an ancient oracle, 'how the Heavens glitter with intellectual sections.' These are archetypal images we follow dimly in our evolution."

"How do you conceive of these powers as affecting civilisation?"

"I believe they incarnate in the race: more in the group than in the individual; and they tend to bring about an orchestration of the genius of the race, to make manifest in time their portion of eternal beauty. So arises that unity of character which existed in the civilisation of Egypt or Attica, where art, architecture, and literature were in such harmony that all that is best seems almost the creation of one myriad-minded artist."

"But," said the indefatigable Leroy, "your world spirit does not merely inspire variety of civilisation in Greece, Egypt, or China, it inspires individuals in the same country to work in contrary directions. How do you distinguish among varieties of national ideals those which have the divine signature from the rest? How do you thus distinguish your inspirations from those of my Dark Angel?" It was as a Dark Angel Leroy wrote his fantasies.

"It is difficult to answer you," said Lavelle, " and if there was a general certainty in human thought I might be regarded as foolish to risk life because of momentary illuminations. But to all of us life is a mystery, and we are like Columbus who was encouraged to venture further on the untravelled seas because he saw a single leafy branch floating on the water. We likewise dare all things if we hear a horn blown from some height of being and re- member that some who lived before us reported that they too heard that horn. We have control over the work of our hands, but little over the working of the soul. But yet we must yield to it, for without it we have nothing. You or I may write some- thing and others will say of it that there is a mastery over our art ; or Rian may design a building all will applaud for its beauty ; but the fountains of thought or vision are not under our control. If vision ceased suddenly with you or me, how could we regain it ? If ideas did not well up

spontaneously from some deep none of us
would know how to trap them, so far beyond
conscious life is the true begetter of thought
or vision. We would appear to ourselves
to have no real being but for the continuity of character of the ideas which well
up within us. Because of this continuity
and harmony we infer some being out of
which they arise. I have come by a round-
about way to answer your question. As it
is by the continuity of character in our ideas
we infer a soul in ourselves, so it is by
continuity and harmony of inspiration in a
race we distinguish those inspirations which
come from the national genius from ideas
which are personal. I came but slowly
myself to see these distinctions, for many
years passed before imagination and feeling
passed into vision and I began to see in that
interior light figures which enchanted me
with their beauty. These were at first
mythological in character and I could not
connect them with anything in the world.
Then I read the history of our nation, and
I was excited by that tale which began
among the gods, and from history I turned
to literature, and it was then I knew the
forms I had seen in vision had been present

to the ancestors thousands of years ago, and ever since they had been in the imagination of the poets. I felt the continuity of national inspiration, that the same light was cast upon generation after generation just as the lamp in that high window casts a steadfast glow and shape on the smoke which hurries past," and he pointed to the ruddy coilings of smoke which flowed by a high building beyond the square.

" What do you mean when you describe forms as mythological in character?"

" There are certain figures which appear continually in our literature, spoken of as a divine folk, apparitions of light taller than human, riding on winged horses, or shining musicians circled by dazzling birds, or queens bearing branches with blossoms of light or fruit from the world of immortal youth, all moving in a divine aether. These were messengers of the gods and through these came about that marriage of Heaven and Earth in our literature which made it for long centuries seem almost the utterance of a single voice. These divine visitations have been the dominant influence in our literature so that our poets have sung of their country as the shadow of Heaven.

The hills were sacred, the woods were sacred, and holy too were the lakes and rivers because of that eternal beauty which was seen behind them as the flame is seen within the lamp. Political thought with us too has been more inspired by the national culture than by the economic needs which almost completely inspire political activity elsewhere. But why should I try to convince you of the reality of national character? Has it not been noted by all who come to us? If we had not been restrained by alien power from control over our own destiny we would have manifested the national genius in a civilisation of our own and it would have been moulded nearer to the divine polity. While all can see the unity of mood and character, I am perhaps alone among you here, though not alone in the nation, in believing it comes from the soul of the world. Such beliefs are perhaps above proof, though we may know the truth after to-morrow's sun has set, falling back into that fountain from which we came."

VII

" I FAIL to see Leroy a harmonious bee in
the divine hive," said Rian, slyly glancing
at that personality. " I remember a temple
wall in Egypt all solemn with immemorial
forms, and some ribald ancient had scrawled
a comic crocodile upon it. Leroy would be
a creator of comic crocodiles in your scheme
of things, Lavelle. I am trying to imagine
him the slave of the inner light. But—"
he broke off laughing.

The other was intellectually indignant.
" I am the slave of the inner light," he said.
" But I do not wish to be the slave of the
inner Lavelle. I do not know why you
delight to see everywhere the echo of a single
mood. I take joy in Lavelle's imagination,
in yours, and in all free imagination, but you
desire to impose your dream on others.
I, if I met a man with imagination like my
own, would turn my back on him. I believe

the emanations of all creatures are poisonous to themselves."

" Well, I am with Lavelle. There could be no place for my art in the world without the aid of others. Architects by themselves do not build cities. Nor would we continue imagining a beauty which could never be manifested. This must also be true of statesmen. They could not go on with the noble labour of civilisation unless there was to be harmonious effort among many to bring it about."

" An idea may be heaven inspired, but is the will to enforce it by violence part of the inspiration?" the historian asked of Lavelle.

" Every idea which arises in the heaven world of consciousness must ally itself with an appropriate force if it is to be born in this world. When we devise anything for ourselves our thought allies itself with force to move the body, and in carrying out what we devise we must often suppress energies and passions which would impel the body to contrary action. So the national genius, if it is to move the body politic, must ally itself with force to overbear what is hostile to it. How else can right find its appropriate might ?   How could national genius create a civilisation if an alien power controls the economic and cultural activities of the people, if it substitutes in youth a mongrel culture for the national culture ?   How but by force can the nation free itself from a power which has taken the sceptre from it, which has killed its noblest children and broken up its laws?   Now, being in peril, it would force us to fight for it, to fight for the power which enslaves us.   So," added Lavelle bitterly, " might a man who had violated a woman, on the ground of this enforced intimacy expect the woman to sacrifice herself for him ever afterwards."

" You spoke of a mongrel culture.   Did you mean an alien culture only, or had you another meaning ?   Do you contend for the superiority of the culture of our nation over the culture of all other races ? "

" Could we argue for the superiority of poet over musician, and having decided this ask poet or musician to express themselves in the superior art ?   No, we realise that natural aptitudes are not interchangeable, and each person must of biological or spiritual necessity practise the art for which he is fitted.   If there be a true national

culture it is best for the nation.   It associates
what is manifested with what is yet un-
manifested in the soul of the country, and
tends to draw down from heaven to earth
a complete embodiment of the divine idea.
I feel it to be true about poetry that it is
born in the dream consciousness and made
perfect there before it enters the waking
consciousness.   If a verse or even a line
I think beautiful sounds in my brain, I know
that by brooding upon it I can draw down
the complete poem.   I think in the same
way when we brood on what is beautiful
in the dream of the ancestors we attract out
of the deeps of being all beauty which is
akin to it.   But to argue about the abstract
superiority of cultures would be to enter
upon a futile controversy like an argument
between ants and bees over their civilisations,
as if those who had the worst of the argument could change their species."

"Yet there are no biological distinctions
between men such as divide ants from bees.
The literature of other races we understand
as we do our own.   Nothing which is human
can be alien to humanity."

"We can draw inspiration from other
races, but their culture can never be a sub-

stitute for our own," said Lavelle. " The
wisdom of others is full of danger, for we
may lose what is ours and break up our
natural mould of mind. A Chaldaean oracle
uttered a warning against changing the
ancient names of evocation in a country
because such had a power affixed to them
by the mind of the Father. A national
culture evokes by association of ideas a
thousand moods which an alien culture,
however noble, cannot evoke because the
symbols and forces referred to are not
always present in us. If all wisdom was
acquired from without, it might be politic
for us to make our culture cosmopolitan.
But I believe our best wisdom does not come
from without, but arises in the soul and is
an emanation from the Earth spirit, a voice
speaking directly to us dwellers in this land.
We are among the few races still remaining
on earth whose traditions run back to the
gods and the divine origin of things. There
have been men in every generation who have
seen through earth as through a coloured
transparency into the world of which this is
a shadow. Hence it comes that our land,
the earth underfoot, is holy ground. In
the earliest mythological tales the sacred

VII THE INTERPRETERS

mountains, lakes, and rivers are named.
And why were they sacred ? Because there,
as on Sinai, men spake with divinities ; or,
starting hence, they were visitors to the
Country of Immortal Youth, and returning
reported of it that it was not far off but near
and it was accessible to all of us. Even
where the literature is unread something of
the tradition remains with the peasant, and
at times he has vision so that he sees in
waste places the blaze of supernatural palaces,
and people look out upon him with eyes
which are brighter than human. He broods
on such things, and in dream he visits the
world he broods on, and there arises from
this a commingling of natures, and a certainty
about spiritual things, and the soul follows
a true path and is not led into the maya of
abstractions. I know there are few now who
travel on the primeval highways of being,
and they have become tangled byways for
most, and are rarely travelled, but still the
way to those who walk in light is known,
and I would preserve what remains of knowledge so that we may continue to draw from
our own well of wisdom. In countries
where they have lost the primeval consciousness of unity with the Earth spirit they either

have no mythology and cosmogony and thought is materialistic, or else they go to Greek or Jew for their spiritual culture. So distant lands are made sacred, but not the air they breathe ; not the earth underfoot. A culture so created has rarely deep roots, for it is derivative, and nobody can climb into heaven by its aid, and it is of such cultures I spoke as mongrel. We find something false even in the greatest masterpieces of such literature. We admire the grandiose style of Milton, but feel his Heaven-world is rootless and unreal and not very noble phantasy. We wander in such literature into many palaces of the soul where there are no windows looking out into eternity, and their beauty at last becomes a weariness to us, for we seem for ever to be imprisoned in personal phantasy, and we come to think there is nothing but individual life and the race drops out of the divine procession."

" The roots of your being seem remote from humanity, Lavelle, though I have heard you move crowds as deeply as Culain. Your heart, I think, you use only on public occasions, but privately its temperature seems a little arctic."

"Were we not to discuss our ideals as between ourselves and Heaven and the relation of our politics to the politics of eternity?" Lavelle defended himself. "I have tried to make clear to you where I think the Spirit breathed in the deeps of my being and what ideas of our destiny arose in me. I do not think I am unconcerned about the quality of human life. Why am I here? Why did I take a part in this revolt? I saw a spiritual culture being extinguished and a materialistic and ignoble culture being imposed on us to the degradation of human life. I believe humanity divine at its root. Out of this root comes beauty, intellect, imagination, and will. Out of this was born everything we adore in humanity. The heroes of our own race, all those we hold in our memory had this half-divine character. They were transparent to spirit. Though I believe with the apostle if we find the Kingdom of Heaven within ourselves everything else will come to us, yet if I had to build up a social order and could not wait for the slow evolution I would begin it with consideration for the poorest first and I would have Culain as my architect."

The Socialist leader, a huge figure half hidden in shadow, had been listening with head bent as if brooding doubtfully over ideas remote from his own but which came by long detours to a sudden harmony in action. He lifted up his head as if he was about to speak, but out of the silence which followed Lavelle's words there came a disdainful voice.

" All this is very well in poetry. Our wives and daughters may read such things in pretty books. But what a basis for world politic ! Such imaginations as these may allure romantic boys and girls, but Nature does not endow them with vitality. The tribal communities are gone behind time irrevocably and are like fossils in human memory."

The prisoners peered into the shadow. The voice came from Heyt, the president of the great air federation who had been so strangely thrust into their company. The world state was here to defend itself from its rebels.

VIII

THE disdainful voice went on: "You are intellectuals, in your political thinking like those mathematicians who pursue the elements beyond aether into mathematical space, and when their calculations are worked out are unable to find the material analogue of the result. You have lost relation to the body politic, and political thinking apart from an organism is futile. The intention of Nature is seen in the forms it creates and not in the dreams of its creatures. The kid which hears a lion roaring may desire limbs of a colossus and a neck powerful to toss like the rhinoceros, but does Nature therefore enlarge its stature? You cry out against the world state which Nature has made like the lion, but the will of the world soul is seen in the organisms it endows with power. The might of an organism is a measure of its rightness, for no organism could grow to power through centuries maintaining itself

against the evolutionary purpose. The up-
holding of a regional ideal is like the display
of a ruined house inhabited by a few shadowy
ghosts. If Nature was with your thought it
would have bestowed power on it, but the
world soul has decreed the world state."

" That decree," an angry voice protested,
" if it ever was made, is now annulled in this
city and over the world," and there was a
clamour of prisoners repudiating Heyt's
interpretation of cosmic purpose.

" Our discussion would be unprofitable,"
said the historian finally, " if it became
merely controversial as to the outcome of
the present conflict. Our fellow-prisoner
was explaining why as between himself and
Heaven he is for a world empire. Should
we not listen to him also, for, if fire falls on
this city from the sky ships, he may be a
fellow-traveller with us to the great Original,
and I think myself in every dream and
hope of man there is some story of the glory
of that King."

" Well," said Leroy, " I am ready to hear
any politic discussed. It would be one of
the finest ironies of life if he converted any,
and they were brought out to die for the
nation having just become initiates of the

empire.   Go on, sir," he said to Heyt.   " I
represent individual as you collective humanity.   Perhaps our extremes may meet."

" How does this power enter the organism
of empire ? " the historian asked of the
imperialist.   " An avalanche gathers power
as it slides down the mountain, and a man
may gather power momentarily from the
summoning up of the baser passions of his
nature.   You will admit power may be
generated in many ways, but you, in your use
of the word, implied purpose and an overflow from the world soul."

" I find the design of Nature in the organisms which have birth in it, and from the
energy which fills them I divine their future
development," Heyt made answer.   " The
power I spoke of does not lie in the generation of mechanical force but in the minds
which organise control.   Nor do I think the
intellectual power which comprehends natural
law and uses cosmic forces low in the scale of
human faculties.   There are many with such
wisdom in the service of the world state.
Why ?   Because their science has revealed
to them the unity of law and the harmony of
power which make the universe a solidarity,
and their politic is to make this unity self-

conscious in humanity. Minds with this idea leap to each other as atoms of the same element leap to each other in the chemistry of nature. I felt what I believe to be cosmic consciousness stirring in myself and others when organising unity of control in the many fleets which had roamed the air. Before that each had brought into an element with no frontiers petty ideas of nationality born in regions bounded by hill, river, or sea. What place has nationality in the limitless sky, and yet the little nations, if permitted, would proclaim territorial rights in the aether up to the infinite. The cosmic consciousness manifests in the world state and to it these tribal distinctions are invisible."

" If you get at a sufficient distance from Earth," said the ironical Leroy, " it also will disappear and need not be considered. At present altitudes only humanity is invisible."

" Humanity has heights and depths which are invisible to each other. It is possible the heights may seem inhuman to the depths," retorted Heyt, equally ironical.

Leroy persisted, "Lavelle interprets cosmic consciousness in a sense contrary to you. I think you both err. I heard a street orator

zealous for souls interpreting cosmic consciousness in his own fashion : ' In that last
dreadful day,' he cried, ' God will flout at
you. He will point His finger at you.
He will say, " Ha ! ha ! " You had your
chance. You would not take it. Now you
will go to Hell ! ' You and Lavelle are
more dignified. You do not create Deity
in the image of the corner boy. But are you
less anthropomorphic in your conceptions ?
You justify the moulding of humanity to
your will by imperialism in the Heavens. I
believe in the intensive cultivation of human
life and think the cosmic purpose is seen in
the will of myself and others to be individual
and free. The cosmic consciousness I conceive to be an autocracy gradually resolving
itself into a democracy of free spirits. You
would make me the slave of a light I do
not see, a law I do not know. How is
cosmic consciousness to be recognised when
it can be so variously interpreted ? "

" The interpretation," said Heyt, " which
is most in consonance with Nature has first
claim to consideration. To men of science
the universe is demonstrably under the
dominion of unalterable and inflexible law.
And it can be sustained in argument that

apprehension of that law is the only light of cosmic consciousness in man. I perceive you hold democratic ideas, but where in Nature do you find traces of democracy to justify you in surmising it in supernature? Do you suppose the heavenly host is a democracy and planetary affairs are arranged in council as with men in some petty commune? If you think so argue it out with the mathematicians."

Every one in this age sought for the source and justification of their own activities in that divine element in which matter, energy, and consciousness when analysed disappeared. It was an era of arcane speculation, for science and philosophy had become esoteric after the visible universe had been ransacked and the secret of its being had eluded the thinkers. Heyt was high in the councils of the world state. On such men as upon deities converged all the forces of protest, and to them also came all that was to be said in support of state policy by the thinkers who, as priesthoods have always done, supported established authority. The prisoners were irritated by his tone as of one speaking from an immense height, who could with difficulty discern the ideas stirring in the world beneath him.   But the historian in his endeavour to relate political moods to their spiritual ancestry went on.

" To perceive law in Nature does not of necessity lead to the conception of a world state.   Where do you get natural or super-natural justification for your denial of freedom of evolution to so many millions ?   On what truth do you rely to balance all that curbing of life ? "

" On the unity of Nature," was Heyt's answer.   " Has not our science tracked the elements back to one primordial substance, and the forces operating in Nature to one fountain ?   Our science in its theory and practice is based on these conceptions.   Our politic in its theory and practice rests also on these fundamental unities.   Through the world state humanity moves upwards to its source and becomes conscious of its own majesty."

" It is the begetter of very bad art," interrupted Rian.   " I refuse to believe there can be truth in the spirit which does not create beauty."

" When the building is well built we may think about the decoration."

" Beauty is not decoration.   If it is not

in the design, if it is not laid with the foundation stone it will never be in the completed edifice. Where there is no beauty there is no spiritual authority. You shall not rule us with that story until the words you cry even in wrath break in a foam of beauty on the ear."

"Possibly," said Heyt scornfully, "you are mourning so much over the ruins which must be removed that the design of the world state is to you invisible. I have no doubt the scrub which withers under the shadow of a great tree can see no shapeliness in the strength which pushes it aside and denies it sunlight. But the decay beneath fertilises the forest. Nature works the material into higher forms. The world state will absorb its romantics and transmute emotion into wisdom. The change of phase is inevitable as the change from childhood to manhood."

"How can the state be an organism in the sense that I am?" cried Leroy. "Is there anything affecting simultaneously its disconnected cells? With us the cells are knit and thrill together. In what sense other than mere metaphor is the world state an organism at all?"

"The state is a true organism because its units exist in an element which is the vehicle of emotion and thought, so that the units vibrate together. Have you never seen an orator by his magic make one creature, of which he is head and heart, out of a thousand people ? Is that unity only brought about by the words he utters ? Do we not know that as water is stained ruby by wine his passion colours the element which bathes his audience so that they vibrate in unison. This is an internal or psychic unity, and by this they become for the moment as much one being as you are. The orator creates a temporary unity. The state creates an enduring unity. Every state begins with some powerful personality more absorbent than others of the element which is the source of power, and he gathers myriads about him as an atom of crystal flung into a bath draws to itself the atoms of that element in solution. The organism so created continues until a higher phase of consciousness is reached, and humanity instinctively turns and regroups itself about the higher power, realising a profounder consciousness in the contact. Human evolution is the eternal revealing of the Self to the selves. In the ancient world the state had the character of the most powerful person in it. The state gradually becomes impersonal through science and the comprehension of Nature whose energies are becoming self-conscious in humanity. Science now sits in the seat of Caesar. It is sustained in power because through it life rises from ignorance to wisdom and it clings to the revealer. I do not think your revolution will shake the unity of powerful minds which control human destiny through the world state. Your ideas are weeds growing in the fields of being and they must be uprooted like weeds."

Heyt paused for a moment and there was a certain grandeur about him as he continued :

" I know that I am part of an organism lit up by a cosmic consciousness which shall rule the world. Humanity has yet to be born from the world egg but it shall be born by the stirring of cosmic consciousness through all its units. It shall control the elements and extend its dominion illimitably through Nature."

" He will next threaten to subdue the Ruler of Heaven ! " cried Leroy, fascinated in spite of himself.

" Yes," said Heyt, turning on him, " we may storm His Paradise ! "

IX

" WITH such ideas," said Leroy gaily, " you
will hardly be welcome in the Kingdom of
Heaven. Though I would myself cast out
from that majesty all souls who would
wriggle in as worms and miserable sinners,
insulting Heaven by their abasement before
it. Here you are an enchanting companion.
In prison you enlarge our imagination.
But you imprison our minds when you are
free. It is true the orator may make a
myriad replica of his own passion out of
those who listen to him. But that does not
prove he is right or they are not fools. The
state may create a more long enduring unity
of mood among millions but it does not
prove that they are not being dehumanised.
They become fractional elements in an
organism rather than complete beings. The
more scientifically efficient is the organism
you create the more does it dominate the
units and remake them in its own image,

75

and when has the mass ever risen to the level of the individual ? Though there be one thousand millions in your world state does it in its totality equal one Shakespeare ? I am with Lavelle in the struggle for national freedom, and if the nation wins I shall fight in it for the freedom of the local community and for the greatest richness and variety in life. Prove to me that your world state is a human organism, that the law of its being is the law of my being : let your multitude in action give me the inspiration I receive when solitary, and I will consider it."

" The culture of the individual ! What is that but images and shadows of happenings in mighty states," retorted Heyt. " The very words you utter are sparks smitten from the anvil of civilisation, and there has been no civilisation apart from the highly organised state. You speak of the law of your being. Do you know what is the law of your being ? You would probably have denied thirty years ago the being you are to-day. Is there any law for you which is not the law of my being and of all being ? Only egomania demands consideration apart from the species. You speak as if the individual mind could be a mirror of infinity."

" It can," said Leroy calmly.

" It cannot be the channel of infinite power," said the other. " If the Absolute could have manifested itself and become self-conscious in an individual would it have created multitudes ? The individual will is not a magnet powerful enough to attract the mighty forces which are becoming self-conscious in humanity. Without these energies operating in the human mind it would be in a state of arrested development —be unable to transmute its vision into being."

" What," asked the old historian, " is the nature of the power you speak of, and how is it to be discerned apart from the individual energies we are endowed with ? "

" The energy of universal mind, the fountain of all the energies in Nature," was Heyt's reply. " It is this we discern in the highest human intelligences and they are conscious of direction. In the great laboratories of the state men seem at first to be absorbed in special studies, but, when they confer later, they find their special labours were only contributory to great discoveries made in common and all had unconsciously worked to one end. We have come to believe every energy and element in nature has intellectual guidance, and the human mind can enter into relation with the mind in Nature.   We are passing beyond the stage where scientist or inventor harnessed Nature energies to a mechanism and tapped them for power.   We are nearing the possibility of direct intellectual control of these Nature energies through a growing comprehension of their relation to their own intellectual guiders."

" It is not science sits in the seat of the Caesars," cried Leroy, " but the magicians. We are coming back in a spiral of three thousand years to the rule of magician and astrologer ! "

" The ancients," said Lavelle, " comprehended and used spiritual powers, but your science only uses material energies.   The ancients attained to a divine vision and saw beauty in its very essence where you only lay hold of some force like electricity."

" If they indeed attained such a vision of the universe," said Heyt, " it may have come by uniting their consciousness with the very force you despise.   I believe this mighty force through all its correlations and manifestations to be guided by intelligence, and that intelligence is the artificer of the universe, of planet and atom, of state and individual alike. The more we understand its operations the more does it enter into consciousness, and the cosmic will reinforces our own. We attain our fullest life by becoming its slaves, for we can have no real being setting ourselves against the cosmic will."

"You conceive then of cosmic mind shaping world history, acting by its intellectual energy on us through a hierarchy of powers and intelligences, and using the world state as its vehicle because it has widest ramifications?" Brehon asked of Heyt.

"Yes. You may so state it."

"The design is to endow humanity with power transmitted from higher to lower?"

"Yes."

"Of course as it is all Heaven inspired it is blasphemy of any of us to question the wisdom of the interpreters of Heaven," cried Leroy, raging. "We know earth history even if we do not know heavenly history. A union of economic federations first strangle national life, then they become international and create world councils and at last dominate everything. Then they discover divine justification for autocratic rule. It is all in the cosmic plan ! You concentrate power in the hands of a few and assert you are endowing all humanity with power and intellect."

" Intellect in any organism must act from some centre," said the imperialist ; " I have not asserted the evolution of society is complete. The body of a child is first animated by childish passions. The being of the grown thinker finally is thrilled by the majesty of law. Humanity as a whole will finally absorb and be moved by those powers which are now the heritage of a few. The power passes from mind to mind linking them by a common impulse or will. If there is revolt against the law the power will overcome it or break it. An allegory of this you may find in the tale of the master who made a feast and invited all to it. When they would not come he sent out into the highways and byways and compelled them with an iron hand. The freedom you conceive of is a chimera. You were born without your consent being asked. Your body, as another here has said, is shaped by a power beyond yourself and you are in it as in a prison.   Only in a little nook in your brain you nourish a fantastic conception of freedom, while every cell in your body, the air you breathe, the sounds you hear, the vision of Nature you behold, stir you with impulses beyond your control."

" I am not certain that I did not, like Ulysses in the Platonic myth, choose my own body," said Leroy, " or that through the labour of ages my spirit did not learn how to build it.   And I am certain it is not for another to dictate to me thought or action."

" You claim too much for the individual from the universe."

" You see too little of humanity for a ruler.   It is easy for you to be slave to your own imagination, and you think it easy for others to be slave to the same imagination, but your world state will be broken upon myriads of wills as rooted in eternity as your own, as passionate for freedom as mine."

" I believe," said Lavelle, " it will be broken by the national will because it tries to blot out the past of nations and would substitute an arid and inhuman science for the infinitely varied cultures which had en-riched the world.   You train men to run a

G

machine efficiently but they cannot guide their own souls. When the labour of their day is over there is a riot of uncultivated senses, Walpurgis nights where everything that is obscene or vulgar meets undisciplined by any memory of beauty. I count it the greatest of tragedies for a man that he should suddenly lose memory so that he could not recollect what songs were sung about his cradle, or the dreams of his youth, or for what ideal he had laboured. And your ideals have brought on many nations the greatest of spiritual tragedies, for they lose memory of their past and do not see the way they came and by what unnumbered dreams they were led. They lose the beauty of poetry, the ennobling influence of heroic story ; and the cavalcades which set out thousands of years before miss their destiny and wander without spiritual guidance in a desert of vulgarity. We have rediscovered our ancient history, language, and literature, our treasure house or paradise of beautiful memories, and we resume the pilgrimage to our own goal. Other nations with us revolt against the domination your world state would impose on them. The river of national life though submerged for a while rises up again. The momentum of a thousand ages, the character and the deep life created cannot be destroyed in a generation."

" The future is as living in eternity as the past," said Heyt. " It is destiny you oppose. Your revolt will not succeed. Too many myriads have been liberated from the tyranny of the past and the narrow prison cells of its cultures which were but the heaping up of fantastic and personal conceptions. The wisdom of Nature which science reveals constitutes a true intellectual culture which knits the whole earth together in a brotherhood with universal Nature. Humanity can now speak one language. Will it return to the past—put on itself the ancient fetters of frontiers, tariffs, and languages which hindered it from a realisation of its myriad unity. I do not think so. Break, if you can, us who brought about a world unity, but you will find you can only continue our work. You must pursue the science of power which has made the skies as native to us as earth to our ancestors, which made unending airways in great spaces, and thronged them with a life which but for us had crawled beneath, or had its movements limited by regional rights. You speak of beauty as if it had perished because of our science, but what beauty ever glimmered in the imagination to equal the vision of earth made possible by our art ? You can leave this city at dawn and see the sun set in the valley of Kashmir at night, and you can, if you will, picnic meanwhile on the Mountains of the Moon. Oh, yes ! to do this we trampled on a thousand prejudices, but we created a magnificence of power earth has not before known. You see above you in air those who keep watch and ward for the world state. At a word they could destroy this city. If they were destroyed a thousand more could darken the day overhead for you or illuminate your night. What power can you invoke mighty enough to overcome that power ? "

" It will be overcome by pity," came in answer the voice of Culain.

X

" THE power of empire," said the Socialist,
" does not descend from any sky god, but
is earth born and sucked up from human
depths where millions pay tribute in labour
and pain. You breathe the magnificence,
but do not feel the agony out of which it is
born. Pity for that human agony has grown
until it has become mightier than empire,
and has marshalled against it armies that
are numberless. There are two among you
here who find inspiration outside the circle
of human life for the deeds they do. But
I believe humanity itself is its own absolute,
and within itself are its own fountains of
beauty and power. Its destiny is to realise
its own nature and the unity inherent in
that being, not a unity imposed from without.
It cannot acknowledge as above its own the
beauty of another being, or allow another
power to dominate it. You look outside
humanity. I look within it and find its

profoundest impulse is to itself.   Lavelle as
a boy began to dream about Heaven and
Earth.   I as a child began a long meditation
about human life, for I was born in a city
of many millions, in the dark heart of it
where the sunlight was grey before it lit our
faces, and the air before we inhaled it had
travelled through long leagues of pollution.
I lived in a tenement crowded with neces-
sitous life, in an abyss where most had come
to the very end of all, where there was
nothing more to be feared and there was that
peace in pain.   It was there I found pity
lay at the root of our profoundest being and
there was a secret joy in self-forgetfulness.
My first thought beyond myself came because of an old woman who wept a quarter
of an hour or so before she died being unable
to rise and give help to another.   That self-
forgetfulness when the self was passing from
life seemed to me to be wonderful.   I have
read poets who sung of fabulous and magic
things, of starbright, clear, immortal drops
of life, and how whoso drinks of that elixir
has never fear of death, nor sickness comes,
nor anything which wounds.   But the life
which forgets itself turns to its true immortality, and in that turning there is a

deeper life than the poets have fabled. The immortality they imagined was but a shadow."

" Oh, it is true, Culain," cried the poet, " it is true, that was the deepest life. We follow too much after shadows for their beauty. But we do so thinking we will become what we contemplate."

" Take care, Lavelle, lest you be dragged out of yourself by your virtues as other people are by their vices," Leroy warned the poet. " Culain exalts pity over beauty or strength. He would lead you by that star into his fold. You will find his humanity has one soul with a single idea which is to sacrifice the many to the One. To sacrifice life ! That would be easy ! But to sacrifice the self ! To do that is to oppose nature, whose purpose is to bring innumerable personalities into being. It was the labour of ages to bring us to be ourselves and it is no duty of ours to hurry away from ourselves."

" To think like that is also to mistake shadow for substance," Culain went on. " You dream you have a rich life when you only have a multitude of ideas. To think is not to live. I believe it is true we become what we brood on, and, if it be true, then

only an image of life can give us life.   On
what should we brood but upon humanity,
the only life we know ?   I too have sat on
the mountains.   The Earth there did not
whisper to me of a life of its own : but
with closed eyes as I sat there came up
before me images and scenes of human life,
not as external things, but as souls they
entered into and burned my very soul, and
I comprehended and felt agonies, aspirations,
doubts, despairs, and striving.   I saw in my
vision that these souls were brighter as they
turned from themselves, and their shining
darkened as they clutched at the personal,
and I knew the shining came because they
were rising to their fount.   That this vision
was of realities I know, for afterwards I
met some I knew first when in an illumined
deep of brooding.   I know we can open
the soul to that innumerable life so that
it can reflect itself in us, and truly we
become it, for it is at its root one being,
one Heavenly Man manifesting in legions
of forms.   I am communist and socialist
because I believe humanity to be a single
being in spite of its myriad forms, faces,
and eyes, and there is only in it such seeming
separation as we find in our own being when

it is dramatically sundered in dream.   Whatever makes us clutch at the personal, whatever strengthens the illusion of separateness, whether it be the possession of wealth, or power over the weak, or fear of the strong, all delay the awakening from this pitiful dream of life by fostering a false egoism."

"You know, Culain," Leroy spoke earnestly, " that I love your mind and heart. You have vision but it is of a life so innumerable that it can only be revealed in the simplest of generalisations.   You say humanity is one being, and you would build on that formula a social order for the whole earth, a social order where everybody possesses everything, and nobody has anything, and the infinite complexities of human nature are constrained into one mould of thought. You have vision and you see infinitude, but you cannot give your vision to those who will build up your communist state.   Your organisation will be to them an opaque idea, an end in itself, not an avenue to the soul. Life by it will be constrained and limited, and there will be unspeakable cruelty to the souls of men.   The greater the organisation you build the more must it be governed by regulation and formula.   It will force on humanity an iron brotherhood, a brotherhood of force not of affection, and that would be the deepest of the human hells ! You offer your candle of vision to the blind. But what use can it be to the blind except as a bludgeon ? "

" All this," said Heyt, " would merely result in a spineless society dominated by vague emotionalism. In every vital organism there must be an element of power. A grandiose conception of society is a worthy aspiration. Love will follow the swift and strong but will not make itself its own ideal. Nothing is sufficient for itself, not even humanity. It must still enlarge its boundaries, because if it feeds on itself it will get thin and weedy like herds where there is too much inbreeding."

" I too think an imagination which is over humanity is engaged in its moulding," said the poet. " Culain, you admit no influence from Nature, though we come out of its womb, nay, are still in its womb. That Nature in which we are bathed is our real nurse. It is she who moulds us in clans yet in infinite variety. When we surrender ourselves to her how full of life we feel ! She transmits to her lovers her own power

of making beauty and whatever is done by
those who live nigh to her is lovely. When
men live too long in great cities the cord
which connects them with the mother being
is cut, and what becomes then is misshapen.
The works of art conceived in cities are
first hectic with the colours of decay, and,
lastly, there is nothing which has not erred
in every line from its natural beauty."

There was a friendship born of ancient
enmity of ideals between Leroy and Culain,
and the latter may have considered it useless
renewing a controversy already plumbed to
its depths between them, for he began a
commentary on Heyt's conception of power.

" What is power ? To be able to move
life as we desire ? We call a ruler powerful
who at a word can fill the sky with armadas.
But what is it moves the ruler ? An emotion ?
a passion ? or a vanity ? And those armadas
which leap into air at his will—what is the
link between them and their ruler but an
emotion ? Such power at its root is only
a unity of sentiment or feeling among many.
What is it has made a hundred million of
workers withdraw labour from the world
state ? What but a feeling, pity for human
life ? Can you arouse a deeper feeling than

pity to compel them to renew their labours ?
I think too that as all human power arises
from feeling or desire so the forces in Nature
if we had knowledge of their mode of motion
are also moved by some desire. Is there a
chemist in your laboratories who could deny
that the affinity between atom and atom was
not an affinity of life with life rather than a
destiny inherent in the mechanism of their
structure ? "

" The will in itself is power," said Heyt.
" The will is the self, the king principle in
our being, and it orders all other emotions."

" In the heroic tales of our people," said
Lavelle, " one story is more famous than the
rest which tells how an aristocracy of lordly
warriors was rent asunder by pity for a beauty
which had been bowed to sorrow by their
king. Beauty itself exercises the most
sovereign power over the soul and the will
bends before it. There is a divine beauty
which is overlord of our being."

" The beauty in humanity is inherent in
it," Culain replied. " As the beauty of a
flower is hidden in the seed cell so the beauty
of humanity flows from its ancestral self, a
mightier Adam or Heavenly Man."

" Do you conceive of that oversoul to

THE INTERPRETERS

humanity as conscious of its unity with its children?" asked Brehon, "or is its consciousness of its unity now lost as we in dream are divided up into This and That and Thou and I, and while we dream have not the sense that the dramatis personae are but one character?"

"I cannot say I know," answered Culain. "I can only say I believe, and yet I feel that that which upholds belief has knowledge. I can argue here and make the plea for a communist state so logical that it is without flaw, and it needs in this world for its completeness no argument drawn from a deeper life. Yet for myself I elect to be socialist not merely because logic and justice unite in the theory, but because of a vision which is incomplete, but which weighs more heavily with me than the most perfect logic. By faith only can I complete the segment I perceive of the vaster circle of human life which includes the Heavenly Man. I know it to be true indeed that soul can have vision of soul, not seeing only as the eyes see, but feeling the being of another as we feel the passion of our own hearts. Because of this the ancient Buddha commanded his followers to meditate with love and sympathy on life in

the four quarters of the world.   This I have
done for many years, and there broke in
upon that meditation, intimate and poignant,
the sense of myriads of lives, and I saw and
felt them as portion of myself, and they
burned my very soul."

He paused for a while as if he hesitated
to reveal himself further, but continued in
his slow speech: " Once at the height of
vision, overwhelmed with that intermingled
life, I cried out in my heart to know its
hope and way and end, and in my vision
these myriad souls became transfigured, and
all, even the darkest of them, I saw as gods,
all shining and ancient with youth ; and a
fire which was within them all seemed to
consume them and draw them into itself and
they fled into it and disappeared or were
melted in darkness and rapture into that
Ancestral Self."

XI

" Why do you speak of pity as the profoundest emotion in such a being ? " asked
the historian.

" There are no words but pity or com-
passion to indicate likeness to that feeling
which indeed is not so much pity as an
emotion of infinite desire, or the yearning
rather of a life limited and divided from
itself for the being it has lost, and which
should be as much itself as the beatings of
the heart. As between myself and Heaven
it was the intuition of the unity of humanity
which led me to become communist. Wher-
ever in history any were born with that
knowledge life near to them reflected it as
in a glowing glass, and there was no fierce
thought of thine and mine. What was the
polity of those who listened to Christ or
Buddha ? Had they not all things in common ? They forbade warfare, for they
would not have the spirit at enmity with

that which was intimately itself, and they would overcome hatred by love. Those who are with me do not arm. We separate ourselves from a social order which is oppressive. We deny it the strength of labour, and when that is denied the old social order with its passionate possessive instincts must crumble. On its ruins we will build a new social order restoring the world to humanity. No one in the new earth will have private property in the earth. There will be nothing to make men feel they have interests distinct from the being of which they are part."

" I do not believe," said Leroy, " if you put devils in Paradise they become angels. If there are any heavens they must be holy only because of things which are imagined there, not because the streets are as fabled of gold or the gates of precious stones. A man may gain his soul by giving up the world, but if his share of the world is taken from him by force it by no means follows his soul will be paid him as compensation. I am sceptical about all methods of achieving spiritual ends by material means. You say there will be nothing in the new social order to make men feel they have interests distinct from the being of which they are part. You will never create such a world. A man can be a glutton upon a crust of bread as well as upon a Neronian banquet, and if he has not great material possessions his vanity will glut itself upon the shapeliness of his nose, or his ideas, or anything else which is his."

"If we bring about the ownership of the world by the people of the world, by the race, not by individuals, such a change is itself evidence the inner attitude of the soul has changed," answered Culain. "The spiritual change comes and must come before the material change. If it had not come the will of the workers would not have been set upon this polity. The collective will acts in this way because its hidden throne is upon this interior unity."

"You believe then," asked the historian, "that in some region of our being we are conscious of unity with that myriad life? Our being here, you say, is dramatically sundered as it is in dream. Is there any sphere where this dream does not dominate the spirit?"

"I believe," said Culain, "in sleep and death we go back to ourselves, and the meanest of us here is there as a god. There

H

have been men at all times who have known this to be true. A great religion based its psychology upon the unity of the soul with all other life in that state which is dreamless sleep to us. In one of its scriptures we are told of a sage who found an outcast sleeping by the roadside, and he hailed that outcast by heavenly names, ' Thou great one, clad in the shining ! King !' and of that outcast he said, so high was his being in sleep he was then like a king moving among his dominions. From that high being men come forth every morning to take up and renew their cyclic labour, which is to make the mightier Adam conscious in all its children, and they of it as their oversoul and very self."

" You think the unity inherent in deepest being must at last become conscious in our life here and express itself in a social order and polity in harmony with itself ? "

" I believe we are evolving to a state where the individual life will reflect in itself the entire being of humanity. The heart will attain its own infinitude of feeling as our eyes have already attained their own infinitude of seeing. They reflect the external universe with its multitudinous forms. The soul will reflect the internal world of multitudinous life. When it has attained this consciousness the polity of earth must be transfigured. Who then would grasp at sceptre or crown or possessions for a self which he knows to be unreal?"

"I do not understand," said a prisoner who had listened with puzzled face to the symposium.

"Never mind, Rudd," said Leroy kindly. "Nothing Culain has said need affect your faith in your leader. It only means his communism is more absolute than any one had ever imagined, and if he has his way nobody will be able to call his soul his own."

"All this," persisted that prisoner obstinately, "seems to be less our concern than the churches. The priests can tell me about God and the next world, if I want to know about them. I expect my leader to tell me how this world is to be made fit to live in. I do not like the mixing of religion with politic."

"The God you heard about in the churches died a very long time ago," said Leroy. "It is centuries since His voice was able to be heard even in a whisper in the sanctuary. It came to pass that spirit fell into matter while matter was ascending to spirit. That means, my dear Rudd, that if you want to understand business in its most subtle forms you must now go to the churches. If on the other hand you wish to understand heavenly things you must now consult the politicals."

" I do not understand," repeated Rudd.

" Well, if Culain's ideas are true you only need to fall asleep to understand everything. Here are two who are now like kings moving among their dominions," said Leroy, pointing to some prisoners stretched asleep upon the floor. He gazed on them with a kind of exasperated admiration.

" I do not know whether I should praise them for their courage or despise them for their indifference to living. Here are the last exquisite drops in the cup of life and they turn down the cup. I never enjoyed life more intensely. It is worth while to take Death as a companion because it brings out all that is most alive in Life. Oh," he cried, " there are some people out there who are living intensely."

A thunder as of some vast concussion in the city smote on their ears. It was followed by a flare which made momentarily a wild illumination in the room. The faces of the

prisoners gleamed in a magic moonlight of
many colours. The sleepers awoke. All
hurried to the windows. The lofty night
was pierced by a thousand circling rays.
The airships were searching the dark above
and below, and the revolving beams made
each appear the fiery hub of a wheel whose
vast spokes rayed out to some remote and
incalculable circumference, and these were
the chariots of gods rolling across the sky.
One of the rays rested on a little mist overhead. It surmised something sinister within
it. There was a vibration in the air as if
a brazen gong had been beaten, and at that
signal all the rays converged on that mist.
Something fell from the cloud. One of
the great airships blazed out as if stricken
by fire and it dropped within the city. A
fountain of flame leaped up where it fell,
and there was another fierce illumination of
the room and of the staring faces of the
watchers at the windows, who all, breathless
and still, were intent on the spectacle in the
sky. Those aerial cruisers, hitherto floating
slumberously over the city, were now in wild
activity. Rising to that higher dark where
their enemy had been hidden, they became
hunters of the heavens. For that solitary

airship of the rebels there was no escape.
Soon it dropped like a falling star. There
came a sigh as of pent-up breath escaping,
and then Rian broke the silence.

" Oh ! that was heroic, that deed of our
comrades. With that little ship to lie up
there waiting for these giants and for death !
That fall ! My heart went dropping with
them. Oh, what was life to them in those
ten tragic seconds ! "

" I wonder," said Leroy, " did consciousness fly from the centre to the circumference,
from earth to heaven ? Or did everything in
their being race to the centre in a mad con-
centration on the self that was to perish ? "

" All physical combats are a nightmare,"
Culain said; " hate, despair, terror, every
emotion called into being suck the soul down
and further away from heavenly being."

" No, no, it cannot be so with these,"
cried Lavelle. " Death was a terror sunken
below far horizons ere they rose on that
adventure. The self had already perished,
for they had abandoned themselves to the
genius of their race and it was captain of
their souls. The last of life they knew was
the rapture of sacrifice."

" I would like such an exit," said Leroy.

" Oh, from all that would crowd on me I think I would know myself truly. While we live, a thought hardly lights the brain ere it vanishes. Our emotions have but warmed the heart and they go. They all hide in caves, and we can be conscious of but the minutest fraction of our being at any one time, never the whole being. I think if I took part in such an adventure the whole populace of thoughts and feelings would rush out of their caves and I could be my entire self if but for a few seconds. Perhaps if they put an end to me to-morrow I may have such an instant looking down a rifle before it is fired. I would not lose it. What I fear is that these airships will wreck the city, and I may go out without a moment to arouse the habitants of my being so that they may all answer the call and I may know myself in death."

XII

"WHAT an epicure of the spirit!" cried
Rian. "The feasts of Heliogabalus are pale
images of gluttony set by this desire to
swallow life in an instant. I hope if I am
shot I will not see rising all at once before
me the cities I might have builded. The
one thing which might make death bitter
would be the thought such imaginations
never could be realised."

"You, like the others, want to externalise
yourself. I want to internalise and be
myself fully. The end of life is to be, not
to do. If your desire is to act, all that is
infinite in you will try to drag others out
of themselves to aid you in your labours.
You will try to build the world in your own
image and there will be no freedom. The
world can only be free when men are content
in themselves and each draws from his own
fountain."

"Many people," urged Lavelle, "are

born under one star and are kinsmen of each other in the spirit and find themselves most truly when they follow together that single light."

But Leroy would admit nothing which subdued the individual to the group idea.

"When you speak of people following one star, all that means is that they are weak enough to surrender their individuality to some more powerful than themselves. Every man must be original or be nothing. Who is interested in the followers of greatness? Were there any Christians worth thinking about after Christ? If we remember any it was because they revealed something in their spirit which was not in the original gospel. No life inspires us because it is like another life. I was once indeed converted to a church, but it was in a dream. I saw a procession in a squalid street in the core of some grimy city, and a venerable old man was there being consecrated as prince of his church. He was adjudged by it most Christlike; and the highest dignity it could confer on him was to name him prince; to give him a garret in those squalid streets so that he might live among the poorest like his Master. In that church of a dream all the priestly work done by archbishops and other dignitaries was entrusted to the newly consecrated, for it was only business. The profound science of the soul was not for youth. I remember in my dream cheering that old man with the tears streaming down my cheeks, and then I awoke and knew it was only a dream and could never happen in life. Though the church endured for an hundred thousand years it would never produce another Christ. I do not believe a second Christ could ever inspire the world as the first did, for time has no story which inspires us when told a second time. The great spiritual clans, the great national clans all try to cast humanity into a single mould. I am against the state as I am against a state religion. Nature in the infancy of the spirit may have been behind the religions and the nationalities ; it may have been in them as the spirit of the hive. But in far ages the time came, I think, when some unknown god whispered to man, ' Now, you yourself, my darling, must create yourself by your own efforts. The universe is before you. Its powers are yours. Take whatever you can.' We are to reverse the ancient process by which

Saturn devoured his children. It is for the children now to devour Saturn, and absorb the universe into themselves individually. The universe is infinite and there can be infinitely varied personalities. If there are differences of character among you it is in spite of yourselves. You are all jealous in demanding adhesion to national dogma, imperial dogma, or social dogma, and you imprison the soul in little cubicles of thought, the soul which might have grown into a myriad wisdom."

"Oh now ! " Rian managed to interrupt the torrent of speech, " you need not be so indignantly individual. I remember a few years ago you had built a civilisation in your own head, and wanted us all to come into it. You were proud of it as Nebuchadnezzar when he walked on the roof of his palace and cried out, ' Is not this great Babylon that I have built ? ' "

"Yes, but I learned wisdom like Nebuchadnezzar. My Dark Angel told me the truth about that myth. The great King found the Babylon he created was only the shadow of himself, and he felt solitary as the man who sees replicas of his own face in a thousand mirrors, and he retired to the simple life.

I escaped from the coils of the net. I live and feed myself on an acre of ground, but I am free and have the universe to roam in thought. I measure men by the magnificence of their imagination, not by the height of their cities."

"What is the universe to roam in if the spirit never meets its own kinsmen ? " cried Lavelle.

"Do you really so love to meet your spiritual kinsmen ? " asked Leroy slyly. "I never found you so happy or animated with them as with Culain or myself. You liked us because of our unlikeness. Confess, dear Lavelle, you were tired of your followers. They never enlarged the boundaries of your spirit but only multiplied ideas you were already familiar with. Should not that lassitude have filled you with terror at the thought that your enterprise might succeed and millions of many coloured characters be dimmed to one tone ? "

"I do not admit the lassitude," said Lavelle, smiling, "nor the terrible character of the uniformity of thought you surmise among my friends."

"Oh, I do not deny minor variations. You permit variety in the little things but

not in the great.   The dogma of the nation
dominates everything and obscures the end
of being.   You are like people who can
only look out on the world through a single
keyhole !"

" You know," said Lavelle, " I do not
think national character or culture is imposed
on men from without by other men, but in
their highest form or spirit are the extension
of divine consciousness into the human.
You will not agree with me in this, but you
will admit there must be identities of thought
or culture among those who live in the same
region, or else chaos or mere anarchy, not
in your sense but in the physical, will
follow."

" Oh yes, we preserve language which is
necessary for communication of thought as
light is for perception of form.   But I do
not agree that there need be more in common
between the souls of men than the spirit
of kindness which reconciles all things other-
wise incompatible."

Here the historian interposed.   " You
said something a little while ago inferring
an original unity for all living things.   You
spoke of the universe as an autocracy gradually
resolving itself into a democracy of free

spirits. Can these spirits divest themselves altogether of any relation to that being of which they are emanations ? What is the relation ? You use language which presupposes identity and yet you affirm separateness. If there be any dependence of your being upon heavenly being, you must surmise that relation for the rest of humanity. And if there be a link of identity of consciousness on some plane of being, this naturally would express itself in life. Do you assume any relation between Heaven and your spirit ? "

" You may think of me as a rebel angel," answered Leroy. " I am in revolt against Heaven."

XIII

"I AM not averse to Heaven. I confess an artist's longing to see the fabled palaces, the gates of precious stones, and the streets of gold which some rail at. What is amiss with Heaven? Is the government oppressive?" asked Rian, laughing.

"Leroy is lapsing into fantasy," said Lavelle. "His Dark Angel will not allow him to be long serious."

"Fantasy!" cried Leroy, "when I utter the thing I hold to be most true, when I reveal myself most, you think I am not serious! I am rebel against the Heaven to which in imagination you are slaves. You all rest on divine powers to which humanity must be subservient. Yet it was to escape from their dominion over the spirit I verily believe a migration set in from Heaven to Earth. You assume it was in the divine plan. Have you never dreamed it might be our own primal will carried us here, that

111

we would not be the slaves of light, and we chose free individual existence full of agony even rather than spiritual passivity.   Do you remember to Dante, overwhelmed in Paradise, Beatrice speaking ?

> What overmasters thee
> A virtue is from which naught shields itself.

When we gaze at the sun we are blinded to all else.   What could the spirit be in Heaven but a mirror of that glory ?   There would be nothing for it but vision and it could have no being of its own.   What wisdom could there be for those who are pure by birth-right, who have not suffered or struggled nor willed in freedom their own destiny? We grow into a myriad wisdom through aeons of pain, and by that wisdom we are higher than seraph or archangel who have not wept as we have nor stayed themselves against the cosmic powers.   You read the scriptures of the world but forget that the seers who revealed the architecture of Heaven told us to fly from Heaven, and that the highest was not there, and it seduced by its sweetness.   Aeons ago the spirit of man revolted against Heaven, but it has forgotten its primal will.   Heaven through the religions and philosophies and through statecraft renews its lordship over the soul so that in all that is done it defers to some divine power. Yet we have in ourselves the seed of something higher than the Heaven you worship."

"The extremes have met!" cried Rian. "The representatives of individual as of collective humanity both dream of storming the Heavens."

"That was the one thrilling thought expressed here," answered Leroy. "But he will never storm the Heavens with an army of slaves. The more the world state dominates humanity the more is the will of the individual made incapable of powerful effort."

"The will grows stronger by self-suppression than in self-assertion," said Heyt. "In the first case it truly overcomes something. In the other desire is mistaken for will, and the man is most driven when he most thinks he is the driver."

"That," said Leroy, "is one of those subtleties which can be uttered in a sentence but which need hours for their refutation. I will say no more than this, that the truth of it depends upon what self is suppressed. I hold your statecraft would suppress manifestation of the deep inner being of man,

I

and when that is overlaid, when you have submission to the world state, there must creep into society that stagnation which is the precursor of death. Whether it be you or Lavelle or Culain achieves the harmony of society individuality must be weakened, and the will lose that diamond hardness which can only be maintained by continuous effort never relaxed for a single instant. If the will be relaxed the powers we should oppose sweep like a tide over the soul and carry it away. We are then like one who has rowed against the stream but who rests on his oars and drifts back and loses all he has gained. I have purchased freedom at a great price, warring against all those who would draw me into an unintellectual harmony with themselves. I give no allegiance to the principles you speak of as the divine beauty or power or soul. If I am swayed by any deity it is some unknown god."

" Your unknown god is suspiciously like the ancient devil," said Rian.

" What was the ancient devil but some still earlier deity, some rebel of the Heavens who whispered freedom to the spirit of man ; who against all external rule urged on it still to persist, still to defy, still to obey the orders of another captain, that Dweller in the Innermost whose least whisper sounds louder than all the cries of men ? "

" Well," said Rian, " it is heroic to defy the universe. I admire even if I cannot follow. For all your prickles, Leroy, you are sweet at heart, and I wonder how all this was born with you. Had you a vision on a hill, like Lavelle ? or did you, like Culain, find your heart the council chamber where humanity met ? "

" We all develop from the first contact of the spirit with the body, and the governing myth in my life was a dream which was born in me as a child. I believe it came from the same primeval consciousness from which welled up the Promethean myth, the legend of Lucifer and the wars in Heaven and many another myth of revolt, that mood in which the many eternally break from the One. In that dream I was one of the Children of Light dwelling in Paradise. Outside that circle were the Children of Darkness, whom we knew not, but they were rumoured to us as dreadful and abhorrent ; and in my dream I wandered away from that Paradise into lonely and interstellar spaces, and I was there overshadowed by some dark divine presence, and I know it was one of the Host of Darkness and I trembled. But it whispered gently, ' We of the Darkness are more ancient than you of the Light,' and of many other things it said I recall this only, ' When most you rebel against the known God, the lips of the unknown God are tenderest upon your forehead.' That, without then understanding, I remembered when I awoke, but because it was the first visitation of the spirit it became powerful in memory and everything in the conscious mind gathered about it, and at last I think that Dark Angel became my soul."

" From such fragile and gentle dreams what mighty movements in the human mind begin ! " the wondering Rian mused aloud. " Lavelle hears a whisper from the Earth spirit in his native land, and it becomes at last a sacred land to him, and he fights as desperately to keep it inviolate as the ancient Jews fought for their holy city. Culain saw some one die who had forgotten she had a self, and he began to remake the world in her image. You hear a voice in dream which hints of something higher than Heaven, and you become the most potent scatterer of revolt against all that men worship. Yes, I can see from the foundation stone how grew up the whole architecture of your thought. Talk of beauty leading us by a single hair! Here is a world in revolt, and three who have each a multitude of followers themselves follow phantoms that none other but themselves may see! O, earth whisper! dream of the heart! Dark Angel! who visited these in childhood, do you know what a storm you have created in the world? I revolt against the evil I see, and I would replace it with a civilisation and social order I see no less clearly in the mind. In the civilisation Lavelle advocates, or in the social order Culain would establish, I see how the means provide a bulwark against the end to which they would lead us. The common mind of humanity can assert itself in council and need go no further. But to what anarchy of life would not your philosophy bring us!"

"I never asserted," said Leroy, " because I protested against human law that the universe itself was without law. If we are true to the law of our being, Nature provides the balance. Let us all be individual, myriad-minded, godlike, acting from our

own wills and our own centres, and will
Nature therefore be upset? No, the law
will adjust everything and bring about a
harmony of diversities. Lavelle, Culain,
and Heyt want to do Nature's work by
providing a harmony of identities. I think
it was old Plotinus who said that when each
utters its own voice all are brought into
accord by universal law. So I have absolute
faith that if we are ourselves fully we do
not become enemies but see more fully the
beauty in each other's eyes."

XIV

A silence followed during which Rian
watched that prisoner of puzzled countenance
who could not understand Culain, and whose
expression indicated that now less than ever
could he relate the politics of time to the
politics of eternity. The sullen eyes, knit
brow, and impatient feet grinding on the
floor, betrayed the anger of one at home in
practical action who finds himself trapped
in a web of incomprehensible abstractions.
The artist nature in Rian, sensitive to moods,
feared some outbreak of exasperated common
mentality, and he turned to the historian.

" Sir, I do not know whether in the long
silence since the completion of your history
you have passed from the self which was in
that book ; whether you have grown apart
in soul from the nation you did so much to
raise from oblivion, and whether we now
seem to you to be vain necromancers in our
endeavour to continue its life. I feel myself

as if the earth was no longer firm under
my feet. All these political ideas which
inspire my comrades appear to be but the
psychic body of ideas descended from heaven,
but which have no companionship with each
other when they dwell in our minds.   Is there
some warfare too in the heavenly house ?
Yet the stars yonder and this earth we trouble,
which are celestial bodies, keep their places
and seem to have no feuds like ours. You
who are older than any here, who have feasted
more richly than any upon the wisdom of the
world, can you effect any reconcilement ?
Here are men who have made themselves
formidable by the imagination and intellect
they brought to bear on the rights of the
individual, or the constitution of society and
the state, who have many followers to whom
they have spoken in the language the
commonalty understand, but what allures
themselves is something they cannot rationalise, something frailer than the laughter of
Helen before which kingdoms faded away.
I begin to wonder whether all desperate wars
in history were not really fought to enable
some fugitive beauty to endure in human
thought. These magicians who have enchanted others, do they weave about their

own spirits an enchantment no more real
than the blossoms of illusion which flicker
under the hands of an eastern juggler ?   I
cannot believe as they believe.   I can divine
a nobler order in the world as the sculptor
divined his statue in the unshapen marble.
But it is this world suggests its own perfection to me, not another world which
would have us fashion this in its own image.
I confess I am frightened to think how
lightly this earth, so solid to my imagination,
weighs with these comrades of mine, so that
if the faintest breathing from another nature
falls on the scales, this earth with all its
state, cities, and history, tilts up as if the
earth scale was freighted with nothing."

    " I think," answered the historian, " there
is some reconcilement of these ideas in my
own being, for they have entered it, and are
in friendly unison ; but I could not now
formulate in any completeness a conception
of cosmic being in which such varied or
contrary impulses are harmonised.   Nor do
I think, even with years of pondering over
a choice of words befitting our imagination,
could words ever represent, to one who has
no direct vision or intuition of his own,
what the words signify.   I utter the word

' spirit ' or ' beauty,' and in my own being these words are symbols of emotion, moods, memories, powers, intricate and intermingled, and so it is with almost everything we give name to. No single mental process, except perhaps the mathematical, has ever been adequately translated into an external symbolism. Speech is not like a mirror which reflects fully the form before it ; but in speech things, which by their nature are innumerable and endless, are indicated by brief symbols. For speech to convey true meanings there must be clairaudience in the hearing. Those who have spoken here have spoken intuitionally and without the laborious processes of logic. I also will say what I imagine in regard to these things, evoking in my mind images and powers, and trusting to the intuition with which you have apprehended each other to see what is in my being also. It may help us to a reconcilement if we remember our infinitely varied human nature when analysed is a simple trinity of qualities. Whatever we do, think, feel, or imagine, whether about ourselves or the cosmos, we think in terms of these three fundamentals, which are matter, energy, and spirit. We can surmise beyond

these nothing except that transcendental state
where all raised above themselves exist in
the mystic unity we call Deity.   In themselves they are as mysterious as Deity, and
when we ponder upon them they allure us
to regions where they become dark and
blind with glory ; so that the solid rock,
melted and transfigured into its ultimate
essence, becomes primordial substance and is
the garment of Deity or mirror of its being,
and, therefore, that ancient beauty which is
the archetype of all other transitory beauty.
The powers which shepherd the elements
our science and intuition tell us spring
from one cosmic fountain.   This is true
also of the powers we ourselves use, for
some who have passed through the Arcana
where the will has its throne found it rooted
in the inflexible and intellectual power which
sustains the universe.   Consciousness also
prolongs itself in meditation and ecstasy into
a vaster being, as Culain has said, and we
do not know whether there is any end to our
being.   All that is substance in us aspires
to the ancestral beauty.   All that is power
in us desires to become invincible.   All that
is consciousness longs for fulness of being.
These aspirations have moulded philosophies

and religions as with Plato and Plotinus,
who conceived of Deity as beauty in its very
essence.   There were Indian sages who
taught that the will when concentrated had
a mastery which extended from the atomic
to the infinite, and, in union with the divine
will, gave man almost an omnipotence of
power.   Other religions again led the soul
to the fount of being and said to it, ' Thou
art That.'   I think these desires express
themselves no less in the symbolism of
politics, so that when one or another quality
is predominant in men or races their polity
tends to create that world order in which
the predominant spiritual quality will have
freest play."

The historian was interrupted by Rian,
who said : "But the spiritual bases of four
political theories have been discussed by us,
and your trinity of qualities omits to find
an ancestry for one of these.   Is it Leroy's
anarchic ideas that have no spiritual foundation ? "

To this Brehon replied : " If we can
imagine this trinity exalted above itself and
existing in a unity, so also can we imagine
natures so balanced that they may be said
to be more complete symbols of the Self-

existent or Solitary of the Heavens in whom
all qualities inhere.   Such men tend to be
self-sufficing and to assert absolute kingship
over their own being.   They exist in increasing numbers ; and the philosophy of
anarchy which they profess, from being the
most despised of political theories has in
three hundred years become one of the most
powerful.   That has come not only because
the right or justice of the individual, which
appeals to the highly evolved soul, is
asserted, but also, I think, because the
creation of great individuals is the intent of
Nature, which it has been said exists for the
purposes of soul.   The external law imposed
by the greatest of states must finally give
way before the instinct for self-rule which
alone is consonant with the dignity and
divinity of man.   Though these are travelling
on the true path I do not think they will
attain their full stature until they comprehend the spiritual foundations on which
other political theories rest, and can build
on them as do the devotees of beauty or
love or power."

XV

" I CAN understand Lavelle, Leroy, or Culain
stirred by the spirit, but the mass of men
seem immovable as rock by that wind,"
said Rian. " I know when I see Lavelle
walking down the street he may be treading
heavenly pavements, and that Culain sees
souls not bodies, but most men walk on
concrete pavements and are themselves but
animated matter. They nurse some dream
of power for their party or profit for themselves, and these desires converge on the
state, and so the world is made which we
are trying to unmake. I can see when
humanity is in a state of flux, as it now is, how
men with imagination spiritually quickened
could create new moulds into which the
molten humanity may pour itself. But you
suggest the spiritual powers at all times
influence the world order, whereas I think
those so influenced are few, and hardly in
a thousand years is the multitude melted

into a spiritual mood. If the divine nature
is so interwoven with our humanity it con-
ceals itself marvellously from our eyes."

" Our philosophy supposes the universe
to be a spiritual being," answered Brehon,
" and if it be so the least creature which
becomes in it cannot escape infection from
that which is its own original. The most
subtle analysis of consciousness brings us
to the apostle who said ' In Him we live
and move and have our being.' We find
that miraculous or transcendental element
involved in the swift creation which takes
place in dream, in the instant and marvellous
harmonising of consciousness with the perpetually varying infinitude of nature, and
minute analysis leads us step by step to the
realisation that the least motion of body or
soul involves this transcendental element.
Nor do we merely exist in this divine nature.
It exists also in us, and I think men ever
follow a spiritual light even when they seem
to be most turned away from it. When we
analyse their desires, even those which seem
gross, we find what allures them is some
beauty or majesty mirrored in this from
a loftier nature. So the lustful man is
tormented by an inversion of the holy spirit

or creative fire. The drunkard thirsts for
fulness of being as the God-intoxicated do.
Vanity in us is an echo of the consciousness
of beauty in the artificer of the cosmos,
while hate is the dark descendant of that
wisdom which is perpetually regenerating
the universe. Even those lost and hopeless
who pursue their desires to spiritual death
are still seeking spiritual life. They follow
a gleam mistakenly as we may imagine light-
demented moths dashing themselves at a
moon on water. As in their private lusts
men still follow something in its essence
universal, so too in their imaginations about
society are they allured by images and
shadows of their own hidden divinity."

"They are all God-inspired then?" Rian
interposed doubtfully. "But how is it if
all depend on the One we are here in conflict
with each other?"

"I think it might be truer to say of men
that they are God-animated rather than God-
guided. Yet in a sense it would be true to
say that of them also. It is not necessary
to infer because there are contraries here
there must be discord in the heavens. We
do not assume Nature is at strife with itself
when there is storm or earthquake, for we

know the elements from atom to mass are
subject to a law from which none can escape,
for it inheres in the being of nature which
maintains through its myriad transformations
music and balance in itself. We can imagine
our own antagonisms also harmonised in the
being in which they exist, and that too by
a law from which there is no escape. The
law at last makes us conscious of itself and
we discover where it constrains us and where
there is freedom.   In this sense if we equate
Deity with law we may be said to be God-
guided. We are free of abyss or height,
but if we descend to the depths the spiritual
powers desert us, as in the Chaldaean myth
of the descent of Ishtar the goddess at
every gate was bereft of some symbol, and
sceptre or diadem or robe or girdle or sandals
were taken from her until at last she entered
the Underworld naked and shorn of divinity.
That was a myth of the soul. To us too
as we rise from the depths the spiritual
powers return as to Ishtar at the gate
of every sphere was restored some of her
regalia, until entering through the Everlasting gate she was once more crowned and
Queen of Heaven. I do not think there
can be finality for us in politic, even in

K

theory, because man is a still evolving being not yet come to his fulness. A change of mood, and what he held to be precious yesterday is no longer so to him, and, un-regretful, he lets it slip behind time. Every high imagination of man is the opening for him of some door to the divine world, and there, like Ishtar, he takes on some new attribute. He may have a vision of beauty or feel the majesty of law, or the love which links the Everliving together ; and as he sees or feels he imagines a world order in harmony. As his aspiration is so is his inspiration. He becomes maker of beauty, revealer of law, avatar of power, dispenser of justice, or seer of the heart. Whatever he has apprehended of the divine nature he wishes that to prevail on earth."

"We cannot live truly by mimicry of things either seen or conceived," interposed Leroy. "It is life itself we ought to exalt. All this would reduce us to some kind of logical existence in which the premiss was not within us but without. If we are to live truly it must be by inward impulse."

"Why do we not walk out of this prison?" answered Brehon. "Because there are walls all about us and a closed door. If there is

immutable law the soul must take cognisance
of it.   Yet, if we consider truly, what is any
vision of beauty but the lighting up in us of
some lordlier chamber of the soul than it has
hitherto inhabited ?   The apprehension of
law is but the growth in ourselves of a profounder self-consciousness.   The mighty is
apprehended only by the mighty, and no
dew of pity ever seemed to fall from the sky
save on those who themselves were tender
of heart.   The universe perpetually echoes
back to us our own attributes, and our
furthest reaching out to understanding of
the nature which envelops us is our deepest
comprehension of our own being.   The
universe exists for the soul, not the soul for
the universe.   We cannot imagine a transformation of the Absolute which could have
meaning to itself, but for the spark wandering
in the immensity of that being we can
imagine endless progress from atomic to
infinite life.   They are wise who study the
architecture of the cosmos, for the heaven
and the heaven of heavens were builded for
us, and that majesty is but the mirror in
which we become conscious of our own
magnificence.   I do not think as you do
that recognition of the divine powers will

take sceptre or crown from the spirit of
man, for all meditation ends at last with the
thinker, and he finds he is what he has
himself conceived.   The poet Blake said :

> It is impossible for thought,
> A greater than itself to know.

So too the Indian seers of old brought the
soul by a thousand pathways to the divine
world, but never allowed it to fall down or
to worship divine being as beyond it, but
whispered it in the ecstasy of contemplation
' Thou art immortal.   Thou art that.' "

" But where are you now leading us?"
cried Rian.   " It is a long way from world
polity to spiritual ultimates ! "

" But that is where all these as they have
revealed themselves are tending.   All their
politic is but a groping through the symbols
of earth to the Kingdom of Heaven.   They
are all citizens of that Kingdom and they
drink in imagination from the same fountain.
Politic is a profane science only because it
has not yet discovered it has its roots in
sacred or spiritual things and must deal
with them."

" Shall we find this Kingdom on earth ? "
asked Rian, " or must we adventure into

another world ?   Must we take the Kingdom
by violence ?   I can understand the logic
of fighting on earth, but if we are truly
seeking for the Kingdom of Heaven, can we
gain it by conquest ? "

XVI

" I<small>F</small> we accept the idea of a divine humanity
brought to harmony in some remote Golden
Age, how can this better us to-day ? " asked
Lavelle. " Must we not still fight for the
good we are assured of ? I believe the
ideals for which men are not ready to die
soon perish, for they have not drawn nourish-
ment from what is immortal in them. If
we do not throw life into the scale we are
outweighed by those who are ready for this
sacrifice. If we become philosophical on-
lookers, our nation, its culture and ideals,
perish, being undefended, and an unresisted
materialism takes its place. The world
becomes less lovely by what is actually
beautiful fading out of human life, not
dying nobly, as it might, overcome by a
superior beauty. The incarnate love came
not with peace but a sword. It does not
speak only with the Holy Breath but has
in its armoury death and the strong weapons

of the other immortals. We cannot put on the ideals of other peoples or future ages as a garment. It is better to remain unbroken to the last, and I count it as noble to fight God's battles as to keep His peace."

" I do not advocate philosophical indifference, for I believe we can be fighters in the spirit and use immortal powers," the old man answered the poet. " In the divine economy nothing is lost, for the spiritual nature exerts always an influence equal to the intensity of its being. You desire things which can only be a possession of the spirit, but you yet act as if they were material possessions which might be lost or stolen. This may be because you have not yet come to understand the laws of that being in which all spiritual adventures take place. I do not think any one can lose what is his own save by descent from the sphere where the things loved have their natural life. I believe spiritual ideals, except for the few who can maintain them through all conflict, are lost if we defend them by material means. There are other ways by which right can find its appropriate might."

" If we could be assured of that we would all be fighters in the spirit ! " cried Lavelle.

" But when did our nation win anything save when it stood armed and ready for the last sacrifice ? "

" You will find," answered the historian, " that every great conflict has been followed by an era of materialism in which the ideals for which the conflict ostensibly was waged were submerged. The gain if any was material. The loss was spiritual. That was so inevitably because warfare implies a descent of the soul to the plane where it is waged, and on that plane it cannot act in fulness, or bring with it love, pity, or forgiveness, or any of its diviner elements. There is another reason why spiritual ideals may not be preserved by warfare, and that is because it is its nature to evoke hatred. Love and hate have a magical transforming power. They are the great soul changers. We grow through their exercise into the likeness of what we contemplate. By intensity of hatred nations create in themselves the character they imagine in their enemies. Hence it comes that all passionate conflicts result in an interchange of characteristics. We might say with truth, those who hate open a door by which their enemies enter and make their own the secret places of the heart."

" That is a terrible thought," said Lavelle.
" But is it more than the expression of an
ethical exaltation beyond human nature ?
Is there not such a thing as a righteous
anger which is proper to us and not ignoble,
nor implicating us in such a tragic fate ? "

" Can there be a beneficent union of what
is good and evil in a single mood ? "

" If warfare indeed brings on us such a
lamentable destiny, by what means may
right find its appropriate might ? You
seemed to affirm that the spiritual powers by
themselves win victories for us. How may
we be made certain of this, for no one will
lay aside a powerful weapon until he is
assured he may exert another equal or a
greater power ? "

The historian made answer, " I came
myself to such a certitude through experience,
being led to brood upon the nature of the
soul, when I was nearing completion of the
history of our nation. Though everything
was done better than I had thought possible,
I felt desolate in spirit, and there came even
an aversion to my work. The light which
had hitherto inspired me seemed now to lead
in a contrary direction. For as one whose
eyes from gazing on vivid orange turn and

rest on a vacancy finds it pervaded by a mist of blue, so my mind began to create in its emptiness the contrary of all I had loved, and the lure of national ideals began to be superseded by imaginations of a world state. Where I might have been led by this reaction I do not know, but that I met and afterwards became one of a company of men existing in many lands who were unknown to the world and were bent on the conquest of that vast life which is normally subconscious to us, so that they might have more than speculative knowledge and be nearer to what they truly were."

" Why was a quest so important pursued in secrecy ? " asked Lavelle.

" It was necessary lest there might be diverted to outward argument and controversy the energies which were all needed for the ascent to spirit, for this quest requires an heroic enthusiasm, a courage rising again and again from defeat with indestructible hope. There was also a wisdom in it, for the mood must be solemn when any would enter the cathedral of the universe. All enmities must be laid aside, as in the East the worshippers lay their sandals outside the mosque. A serenity of feeling in which

all diversities are harmonised has to be
attained, so that out of many a new being
which can act with power might be created.
In that psychic unity the faculties of each
one in the group gradually became the
possession of all, a possibility which Culain
has already apprehended ; and the will of
many in unison was powerful enough to
transcend the bodily life so that in meditation
together consciousness rose like a tower into
heaven, and we were able to bring back some
knowledge of the higher law."

" Was there not peril in this meditation
that the most powerful character might
impose his imagination upon the rest ? "
asked Leroy.   " An Indian faquir can impose
his mental fantasy upon a crowd so that they
will see him swallowing a poisonous snake
which exists only in his imagination and their
vision.   And this would be easier with
groups such as you describe stilled to one
intent and porous to each other's emanations."

" Of this, too, we were aware," said
Brehon.   " For we were guided by ancient
wisdom, an experience garnered through
generations.   It is true that the purification
of nature, obligatory if we were to succeed,

makes the psyche sensitive and translucent so that the feelings and imaginations of others affect it swiftly, but the will at the same time is quickened to more intense activity and made positive, so that to perceive or receive the emanations of others is not to be overcome by them. It is because I was in so close a psychic unity with others, and that in a brotherhood which existed in many lands, that I was made certain feeling and imagination radiate their influence to the boundaries of the world soul as stars shed their light through space. These influences pour on us and through us and illuminate or darken our lives. I have come to believe even the solitary or captive can by intensity of imagination and feeling affect myriads so that he can act through many men and speak through many voices. The deeper the being the more powerful are its radiations. So far as the intellectual transcends the physical so does the spiritual transcend the intellectual. The avatars of the spirit, the Christs and Buddhas, do more by single gentleness than conquerors with armies do, and build more enduring kingdoms in the spirit of man. The devotees of the spirit, though few, give

XVI THE INTERPRETERS

light to many. With them the deed is done
when the thought is born, for if it is of the
spirit it has more than the swiftness of light,
and a deeper penetrative power, and it
illuminates many hearts which have as yet
no light of their own. If a kingdom is won
by force it must be sustained by force, and,
as Leroy has said, there is no real freedom.
But if there is reliance on spiritual law, if
we seek to be truly ourselves, we draw others
naturally to seek for a like fulness of their
own being."

" Our civilisations have not been built
up by the spiritual imagination acting alone,
but by manifold labours of mind and body,"
said Rian. " I can imagine a house, but
who could live in the house of my dream
unless the builders remake it in the substance
of this world? If poets or music makers
never went beyond the ecstasy of conception
or brought down from heaven what they
had seen or heard, would not our life be the
poorer? Would we have any civilisation
at all ? "

" We do not lessen the power of the outer
man by increasing the power of the spiritual
man, for the spirit cannot be quickened
without the strength of imagination and

intellect being also increased. Nor can the life of man be spiritual only, for he must oscillate between Heaven and Earth until he has reached his own centre and the immortal stills all in its own being. Until we can act from our own centre our ascents to Heaven involve reactions to outward life, but the soul returns to Earth, wrapping its memories of Heaven about it like a cloth, and shining as Moses going down from the Holy Mount. Its deeds then are of a lordlier character and reflect the magnificence of its imaginations. As men come nigher to the immortal their civilisations will transcend ours as the Parthenon transcended the huts of those who herded their flocks in a more ancient Attica."

XVII

" ALL distinctions of nationality seem to
dissipate in a haze in this transcendental-
ism," Lavelle protested. " I mistrust the
philosophy which universalises overmuch.
I admit a being which is the fountain of all
being, but what emerges from that fountain
is diversity of beauty in nature and humanity.
You spoke of ancient Attica.   We find there
as in Egypt, China, India, and other lands, a
character in the culture which does not
appear elsewhere, and this, I think, arose
because the more sensitive minds in every
country came into contact with archetypal
images of a nature peculiar to these regions
of the earth.   If for every man on earth
there is a divinity in the heavens who is his
ancestral self, should there not also be a
varied and diviner nature overshadowing
this earth we know and influencing it as
the soul the body ?   The ancients spoke of
a many - coloured earth above this and

temples wherein the gods do truly dwell, and may not these be the archetypes of our civilisations and the spiritual basis of nationalities ? I must believe there are differences above as below. When we come to our own immortal it cannot be that we cease to have individual character. We cannot in the perfection of the spirit be only perfect images of each other. I believe also in the heaven of which earth is a shadow there are the divine originals of the lands we know. Is not this what was meant by the saying, ' In our Father's House are many mansions ' ? As I listen to you these diversities of beauty and culture which have enriched the world, which have, as I think, their root in a deeper being and should be defended as part of the divine polity, all seem to fade before some gigantic and undefined ideal. Must national distinctions be lost, and if so to what world order are we tending ? "

" I think," said the old man, " we are evolving through all our activities, through politics as through the arts and sciences, to realisation of our full human stature, and in that realisation nothing that is rightly related to our humanity can be lost, no spiritual

influence from earth or sky. If those influences you speak of are Heaven-born, the
more humanity is transparent to spirit the
more will life be penetrated by them. An
oracle of the Oversoul states the law, ' Seek
first the kingdom of Heaven and everything
else will be added to you.' How by this
quest may we attain so rich a being? Because
as the psyche evolves, and we become ourselves more fully, we awaken and attract all
the powers and elements which are akin to
our expanding consciousness. As we absorb
so we radiate influences equal to our intensity of life. We have not yet come to
the limit of our faculties. There are un-
charted regions of psychic nature to which
the perfected faculties give us access and
which we may aspire to rule. The ear has
not attained that infinitude of hearing in
which sounds not only human but celestial
are apprehended. The heart has not attained its infinity of feeling, nor the intellect
its full power of penetration, nor has the
will yet found its conscious root in the power
which sustains the cosmos. With those who
recognise this incompleteness there can be
neither certainty nor finality in the relation
of existing human groups to each other.

L

But to you who have gone beyond the bodily life and have apprehended a spiritual nature I would point out a more excellent way than conflict. There is a justice, a law, which operates beneath all physical appearances. It is this which has brought us together to-night. It was spiritual affinity, not the power of empire, which constrained us, though the law may use material agencies to carry out its decrees. The forces which shut us in whether they know it or not are the servants of that law which shapes outward circumstance in harmony with inward nature. Because life is so moulded for all of us there is no way of bringing about the perfecting of human relations other than by the transfiguration of the individual. Everything we do unaccompanied by an evolution of our consciousness to a higher being is but futile readjustment of surfaces. However we toil, alter, or build we can give nothing more than is in ourselves, and at the close of our ceaseless multiplication the total remains the same. I rely absolutely on this justice in the universe. I will not protest against anything which happens to me, because that would be to protest against my kingship over my own destiny. I am moved here and there by what I am. If there is pain to me in these happenings I shall try to discover where there was misdirection of will which brought it about. Those who begin to live consciously in the spirit must be guided by an ethic based on the nature of the ancestral self or heavenly man. In that being, as Culain has said, all human life is reflected, so that none can be our enemies, and we can overcome only by the fierce and tender breath of love, if love be the heavenly name of that which yearns in us to be intimate with the innermost of all life. Once that spiritual awakening has begun for any the old life should be over, and they should no longer be concerned in the politics of time, and should leave the life of conflict and passion and fit themselves for the politics of eternity. Men cling because of old habit to formulae they have really outgrown and which have lost their lure. Below the old ideals vaster desires spring up, to win mastery over the elements, to chase the divinities. For a time they try to achieve the new ends by the old methods. But it is in vain, for nothing can be won save by the full devotion of the heart. If we do not enlarge the political

ideals with the expanding spiritual consciousness, if we shut any out of our heart
by making emotional or intellectual boundaries to human brotherhood, if any race or
class is excluded, we pervert the spiritual
energies whose natural flow is from each
to all ; and these energies, diverted from
their natural goal, turn backwards and
downward, and poison the very deeps of
life, and they there generate spiritual
pestilences, hates, frenzies, madnesses, and
the sinister ecstasy making for destruction
which is the divine power turned to infernal
uses. Through ignorance of spiritual law
idealists who take to warfare are perpetually
defeated, for they do not realise the dark
shadow which follows all conflict and which
must follow this present conflict by the per-
version of spiritual forces. These perverted
energies endanger human life, not merely
because they lead men to conflict with each
other, but because they bring about a warfare
of nature on humanity. We have supposed
of the Universe it is a spiritual being, and
the elements have intellectual guidance. The
possibility of direct control of these nature
forces through a growing comprehension of
their relation to our own intellectual being

has been referred to here. These powers await our sovereignty. There are legions of allies for us in air, in earth, in sea, ready to do our bidding when we come to our full stature and can command them with wisdom and power. But it is an error, I think, to suppose of them that they are not moved by us now, for there is perpetual communication between the elements in our being and their counterparts in nature. If we poison or infect them by our frenzies and passions, the distraught powers bring about cataclysms, earthquakes, and subsidences, and the evil humanity is shaken off the back of nature. The old poet who said, ' There is not a breathing of the common wind that will forget thee,' was wiser than he knew. We ray our influence not only on each other but on Nature, which more slowly, but inevitably, operates her own justice. Who can say there was no conscious intent in Nature when Atlantis sunk under water ; who can say our mad humanity is not making inevitable a similar doom for this continent ? I say that for those whose spiritual nature has awakened the old life should be over and they should be the fighters in the spirit and use immortal powers. Nor need there

be fear lest by this re-direction of energy
strength should be lost to any cause which
has a basis in the spirit. In the ascent to
Heaven, as Socrates said, we create a multitude of high and noble thoughts, our own
nature expanding until at last we attain a
science which is equal to a beauty so vast.
Our science tells us that the impact of a
heavenly body on the sun makes it to glow
with a fiercer heat. Even so when the soul
ascends to the spiritual sun a more blinding
radiance is emitted from that being. It is
the benediction on Earth for yielding to
Heaven the things which are Heaven's, and
this benediction falls on the path by which
the soul had mounted upwards, and it
illuminates and strengthens what it touches,
the power as it flows outward following the
chain of thought and mood by which the
soul had ascended. Indeed the soul is perpetually receiving this benediction, for, as
I said, every imagination of man is the
opening or the closing of a door to the
divine world, and in whatever way he truly
approaches it it meets him. From that
being in which he lives and moves a light
enters through every transparency, however
momentary, of his nature, and it extends

itself through all that is akin to it. That
which enters us is the sap of the eternal
sacred tree whose roots are in the heavens
and whose branches grow downward to earth.
Whatever way we approach it it answers
us. It entered into Lavelle as a boy upon
his mountain, and was with Culain in his
dark streets, and with Heyt in his state
laboratories and thought of a demiurgic
power, and with Leroy in his passion for
freedom. It endows one with power and
bestows abundantly of life on another, and
to all who make sacrifice it responds by a
law which is so wonderful that if it was
understood it would be the delight of the
heart. I do not think of it as law. I call
it rather Own-Being. The yearning of our
innermost life is for that sweet and stern
and infallible justice, which brings us to
Heaven or Hell as our desires rise or fall
in the scale of being. We are the children
of Deity, and with us consciousness extends
from the dim flicker in heart or brain up
to the Heaven of Heavens. We live in
many worlds, but the links are lost between
the divided portions of our manifold being
so that we forget in waking what we were
in dream, or what majesty was ours in the

regions beyond dream. While we are on this earth matter conditions energy and dominates life. In the mid-region which we also inhabit energy or desire is the master and mind and matter its slaves. But in that heaven world in which man attains his full stature the soul is master, and whenever it imagines or wills the energies and elements act in obedience to it. Those who would mould life in accord with divine nature must remember until their faculties are perfected they look at it through the stained glass of the personal, and be watchful lest they limit in imagination that which is boundless. They must equal themselves to its vastness, for does not the Scripture say, ' Be ye perfect even as the Father in Heaven is also perfect '? Those who seek for beauty will never master its magic unless they also have power, and those who seek for power will find that the mighty surrenders itself fully only to that which is most gentle ; and we shall be re-pulsed perpetually until we have made perfect in ourselves those elements out of which both we and the universe are fashioned and which, made pure, will relate us to the vaster life of the cosmos. Therefore we ought to regard none who differ from us

as enemies, but to contemplate them rather
with yearning as those who possess some
power or vision from which we are shut
out but which we ought to share. If we
seek for the fulness of being there can be
no decay of what is beautiful in the world,
for what is right always exercises its appropriate might. If we do not realise this
it is because we do not know the sum total
of our character and what uncomprehended
elements in ourselves and others defeat what
is noblest. But if we seek for the highest
in ourselves and have this reliance on the
law to justify and sustain us we shall see the
Kingdom. Yes, we shall rule in the Kingdom."

" It seems easy," said Rian, " to reshape
the world simply by going on thinking and
imagining and leaving to others the execution
of what we devise. I do this in my own
art, but the philosophy seems to have a
kind of incompleteness when applied to the
shaping of human destiny."

" It is not easy," answered the old man.
" To cross that red mid-region between
heaven and earth is to undertake labours
greater and more painful than these fabled
of Hercules. In that red mid-region the

martyrdom of the passionate soul, its cruci-
fixion in the spirit, takes place, until all that
is gross is etherealised and it yields itself
finally in absolute resignation to the ancestral
being.   It is not easy to stay the will against
the desire of the world or to draw ourselves
from the attraction of that magnet, as Leroy
knows.   But if we persist a time comes
when the spiritual outweighs the bodily
with us, and it will be so with all men, and
finally they will, at first with pain, but in the
end with rejoicing, journey in multitude to
the Land of Promise.   They will do so
because man is spiritual at the root and
cannot escape from himself for ever, and
the promise of the spirit to the spark wandering in the immensity of its own being was
' I will not leave thee nor forsake thee ' ! "

XVIII

LEROY, a very sincere, but rarely a solemn being for long, grew restless towards the close of Brehon's commentary on the symposium, and broke a rather strained silence with one of his whimsies.

" I once had a vision of a funeral service in the other world before I was born, where I was committed to the grave of this body, and the angelic being who presided murmured something about his hopes for a joyful resurrection of their brother who was now buried in matter. But I felt there was little real confidence in his voice, and when he departed I heard a dialogue between a sceptical spirit who said he did not believe any came back from Earth to Heaven. He had met none. The other spirit, more credulous, thought there was good evidence that certain beings had risen out of the grave of the body, but the sceptic said if they had they were merely cases of premature burial. I have felt while I listened to you all I was prematurely buried myself and was still under that ancient domination of Heaven from which I hoped I had escaped."

" Oh, you need not be afraid," cried Rian. " Your egomania is so concentrated it will persist when all the rest of us have gone back into the primeval silences, and you will be a solitary of the universe wandering about in quest for something to revolt against."

" Well ! " said Leroy, " let us discover who are truly human. What do you think of all this ? " He turned to Rudd, and that prisoner, long baffled in his efforts to understands things remote from his mentality, and at last irritated, broke out with much profanity that he never heard so much folly. One world was enough for him ; one small country all he could think about. The empire found half a world too big to govern. It could only hold together by exterminating any who did not submit to it. If he had to comprehend three worlds before he could act in this he would go mad. He hated being bullied in the name of a law he had no share in making. He hated being instructed how to live in the name of science which was unintelligible, and most of all he hated being told in the name of God how to think. And after this, and much else, he walked indignantly to the other end of the room.

"I have much sympathy with Rudd," said Rian. "He expresses emotions we have all shared, and which, I fancy, had as much to do with bringing us here as these fine imaginations of the Oversoul. I cannot think of him as influenced by beauty or any of the other divinities. I think he belongs to your household, Leroy."

"I accept him."

"How did you come to share in this, Mara?" Rian asked another prisoner.

"Oh, because I wanted to be with Lavelle and you," was the answer.

"I am afraid that is the mob instinct. It is a sub-species of Culain's mood. You lose your identity in that of others. What drew you to fight, Owen?"

"I wanted excitement, I am afraid. I never felt really alive until I was body and soul in our conspiracy."

"It was the same mood which drew Leroy out of Paradise millenniums ago. What was your inspiration, Gavin?"

" I think the thought of death for our country was sweet to me."

" Ah, your emotions must seem lovely to you before you are stirred by them. You comrade dimly with Lavelle. And you, Morane ? "

" I was in a rage with life, I think."

" That rage with you, I know, rose out of pity. You were born under the same star as Culain. And you, Brugha ? "

" I heard rebellion talked since I was a child. It was so with my family for generations. They were in every insurrection. It is a tradition with us."

" That is ancestor worship. I could not place you in any of our categories unless I knew the mood of the first ancestor. He may have been another Leroy. The others are asleep and I am not going to waken them for the purpose of this symposium. It comes to an end. I wonder if I had heard all this a year ago would it have made any difference. It can make little difference now."

A silence came over the room. Rian, who sat on the floor, watched Lavelle, who was in one of the windows. He saw after a while the dark head begin to nod, the lips

to move and murmur.   Being himself tired,
he wondered at the inexhaustible energy of
mind which could so pursue beauty, for he
knew by the movement of head and lips
the poet had returned to his art.   Lavelle
began writing on a scrap of paper in the
dim light, and when he had finished Rian
came and sat beside him.

"Your imagination is a river running for
ever," he said.   "What is it you write?
I hope it is not a swan-song."

"I was completing the last poem in a
Book of Voyages wherein I, like the poets
of our country before me, tell of journeyings
to the Land of Immortal Youth."

"We may soon be travellers there ourselves if all that legend relates of the other
worlds be true.   I myself only wanted to
make this world lovely.   I never tried to
scale the heavens to look on another beauty.
But I would like to hear the adventures of
your voyager."

"It is a dream about one who died in an
old insurrection of our people hundreds of
years ago.   I had thought it finished, but I
was moved by what was said here to-night
to add some interpretation to the dream."

Lavelle's lips moved soundlessly for a

little as if he was trying to find if memory ran easily, and then, in a voice low at first but which soon became rich and vibrant, he chanted the story he had imagined of Michael, a voyager to the Heaven World. Leroy, Rian, and the old historian alone listened, for the others had composed themselves to sleep, which they did soon, being weary, and Culain sat with his head bowed on his arms on the table, and none knew whether he was in a sleep or was meditating.

XIX

MICHAEL

A WIND blew by from icy hills,
Shook with cold breath the daffodils,
And shivered as with silver mist
The lake's pale leaden amethyst.
It pinched the barely budded trees
And rent the twilight tapestries :
Left for one hallowed instant bare
A single star in lonely air
O'er stony lanes the bitter wind
Had swept of all their human kind.

Ere that the fisher folk were all
Snug under thatch and sheltering wall,
Breathing the cabin's air of gold,
Safe from blue storm and nipping cold.
And, clustered round the hearth within,
With fiery hands and burnished chin,
They sat and listened to old tales,
Or legends of gigantic gales.
Some told of phantom craft they knew
That sailed with a flame-coloured crew,

And came up strangely through the wind
Havens invisible to find
By those rare cities poets sung,
Cresting the Islands of the Young.

How do the heights above our head,
The depths below the water spread,
Waken the spirit in such wise
That to the deep the deep replies,
And in far spaces of the soul
The oceans stir, the heavens roll ?

Michael must leave the morrow morn
The countryside where he was born ;
And all day long had Michael clung
Unto the kin he lived among.
But at some talk of sea and sky
He heard an older mother cry.
The cabin's golden air grew dim :
The cabin's walls drew down on him :
The cabin's rafters hid from sight
The cloudy roof-tree of the night.
And Michael could not leave behind
His kinsmen of the wave and wind
Without farewell.   The way he took
Ran like a twisted, shining brook,
Speckled with stones and ruts and rills,
'Mid a low valley of dark hills,
And trees so tempest-bowed that they
Seemed to seek double root in clay.

At last the dropping valley turned :
A sky of murky citron burned.

Above through flying purples seen
Lay pools of heavenly blue and green.
From the sea rim unto the caves
Rolled on a mammoth herd of waves.
While all about the rocky bay
Leaped up grey forests of wild spray,
Glooming above the ledges brown
Ere their pale drift came drenching down.

Things delicate and dewy clung
To Michael's cheeks.   The salt air stung.
From crag to crag did Michael leap
Until he overhung the deep ;
Saw in vast caves the waters roam,
The ceaseless ecstasy of foam,
Whirlpools of opal, lace of light
Strewn over quivering malachite,
Ice-tinted mounds of water rise
Glinting as with a million eyes,
Reel in and out of light and shade,
Show depths of ivory or jade,
New broidery every instant wear,
Spun by the magic weaver, Air.

Then Michael's gaze was turned from these
Unto the far, rejoicing seas,
Whose twilight legions onward rolled,
A turbulence of dusky gold,
A dim magnificence of froth,
A thunder tone which was not wrath,
But such a speech as earth might cry
Unto far kinsmen in the sky.

The spray was tossed aloft in air :
A bird was flying here and there.
Foam, bird, and twilight to the boy
Seemed to be but a single joy.
He closed his eyes that he might be
Alone with all that ecstasy.

What was it unto Michael gave
This joy, the life of earth and wave ?
Or did his candle shine so bright
But by its own and natural light ?
Ah, who can answer for what powers
Are with us in the secret hours !
Though wind and wave cried out no less,
Entranced unto forgetfulness,
He heard no more the water's din ;
A golden ocean rocked within.
A boat of bronze and crystal wrought
And steered by the enchanter, Thought,
Was flying with him fast and far
To isles that glimmered, each a star
Hung low upon the distant rim,
And then the vision rushed on him.

The palaces of light were there,
With towers that faded up in air,
With amethyst and silver spires,
And casements lit with precious fires,
And mythic forms with wings outspread,
And faces from which light was shed.
High upon gleaming pillars set,
On turret and on parapet,

The bells were chiming all around
And the sweet air was drunk with sound.

Too swift did Michael pass to see
Ildathach's mystic chivalry
Graved on the walls, its queens and kings
Girt round with eyes and stars and wings.
The magic boat with Michael drew
To some deep being that he knew,
Some mystery that to the wise
Is clouded o'er by Paradise.
Some will that would not let him stay
Hurried the boat away, away.
At last its fiery wings were still,
Folded beneath some heavenly hill.
But was that Michael light as air
Was travelling up the mighty stair ?
Or had impetuous desire
Woven for him that form of fire,
Which with no less a light did shine
Than those with countenance divine,
Who thronged the gateway as he came,
Faces of rapture and of flame,
The glowing, deep, unwavering eyes
Of those eternity makes wise.
And lofty things to him were said
As to one risen from the dead.
What there beyond the gate befell
Michael could never after tell.
Imagination still would fail
Some height too infinite to scale,

Some being too profound to scan,
Some time too limitless to span.
Yet when he lifted up his eyes
That foam was grey against the skies,
That same wild bird was on the wing,
That twilight wave was glimmering.
And twilight wave and foam and bird
Had hardly in his vision stirred
Since he had closed his eyes to be
Of that majestic company.

And can a second then suffice
To hurry us to Paradise ?
What seemed so endlessly sublime
Shrink to a particle of time ?
Why was the call on Michael made ?
What charge was on his spirit laid ?
And could the way for him be sure
Made by excess of light obscure ?
However fiery is the dream,
How faint in life the echoing gleam !
And faint was all that happed that day
As home he went his dreamy way.

And now has Michael, for his share
Of life, the city's dingy air,
By the black reek of chimneys smudged
O'er the dark warehouse where he drudged,
Where for dull life men pay in toll
Toil and the shining of the soul.
Within his attic he would fret
Like a wild creature in a net,

And on the darkness he would make
The jewel of a little lake,
A bloom of fairy blue amid
The bronze and purple heather hid ;
Make battlemented cliffs grow red
Where the last rose of day was shed,
Be later in rich darkness seen
Against a sky of glowing green.
Or he would climb where quiet fills
With dream the shepherd on the hills,
Where he could see as from high land
The golden sickle of the sand
Curving around the bay to where
The granite cliffs were worn by air,
And watch the wind and waves at play,
The heavenly gleam of falling spray,
The sunlit surges foam below
In wrinklings as of liquid snow.
And he could breathe the airs that blew
From worlds invisible he knew :
How far away now from the boy !
How unassailable their joy !

" Oh, Lavelle ! Lavelle ! " cried Rian,
" I know those hills and little lakes.   Shall
we ever see them again ? "

So Michael would recall each place
As lovers a remembered face.
But, though the tender may not tire,
Memory is but a fading fire.

And Michael's might have sunken low,
Changed to grey ash its coloured glow,
Did not upon his hearing fall
The mountain speech of Donegal,
And that he swiftly turned to greet
The tongue whose accent was so sweet ;
And found one of that eager kind,
The army of the Gaelic mind,
Still holding through the Iron Age
The spiritual heritage,
The history from the gods that ran
Through many a cycle down to man.
And soon with them had Michael read
The story of the famous dead,
From him who with his single sword
Stayed a great army at the ford,
Down to the vagrant poets, those
Who gave their hearts to the Dark Rose ;
And of the wanderers who set sail
And found a lordlier Innisfail,
And saw a sun that never set
And all their hearts' desires were met.

How may the past, if it be dead,
Its light within the living shed ?
Or does the Ever-living hold
Earth's memories from the Age of Gold ?
And are our dreams, ardours, and fires
But ancient unfulfilled desires ?
And do they shine within our clay,
And do they urge us on their way ?

As Michael read the Gaelic scroll
It seemed the story of the soul ;
And those who wrought, lest there should fail
From earth the legend of the Gael,
Seemed warriors of Eternal Mind,
Still holding in a world grown blind,
From which belief and hope had gone,
The lovely magic of its dawn.

Thrice on the wheel of time recurred
The season of the risen Lord
Since Michael left his home behind
And faced the chilly Easter wind,
And saw the twilight waters gleam
And dreamed an unremembered dream.
Was it because the Easter time
With mystic nature was in chime
That memory was roused from sleep,
Or was deep calling unto deep ?
The Lord in man had risen here,
From the dark sepulchre of fear,
Was wilful, laughing, undismayed,
Though on a fragile barricade
The bullet rang, the death star broke,
The street waved dizzily in smoke,
And there the fierce and lovely breath
Of flame in the grey mist was death.
Yet Michael felt within him rise
The rapture that is sacrifice.
What miracle was wrought on him,
So that each leaden-freighted limb

Seemed lit with fire, seemed light as air ?
How came upon him dying there,
Amid the city's burning piles,
The vision of the mystic isles ?
For underneath and through the smoke
A glint of golden waters broke :
And floated on that phantom tide,
With fiery wings expanded wide,
A bark of bronze and crystal wrought
And steered by the enchanter, Thought.
And noble faces glowed above,
Faces of ecstasy and love,
And eyes whose shining calm and pure
Was in eternity secure,
And lofty forms of burnished air
Stood on the deck by Michael there.
And spirit upon spirit gazed,
And one to Michael's lips upraised
A cup filled from that Holy Well
On which the Nuts of Wisdom fell.
And as he drank there reeled away
Vision of earth and night and day,
And he was far away from these,
Afloat upon the heavenly seas.

"Here the voyage as I had written it ended," said the poet. "But I have added what follows in interpretation, for indeed I was moved by what was said in this room."

"Are you at this hour forgetting your own ideals ?" asked Rian.

"You shall judge," answered Lavelle,
continuing his narrative.

I do not know if such a band
Came from the Many-Coloured Land :
Or whether in our being we
Make such a magic phantasy
Of images which draw us hence
Unto our own magnificence.
Yet many a one a tryst has kept
With the immortal while he slept,
Woke unremembering, went his way.
Life seemed the same from day to day,
Till the predestined hour came,
A hidden will leaped up in flame,
And through its deed the risen soul
Strode on self-conquering to the goal.

This was the dream of one who died
For country, said his countryside.
We choose this cause or that, but still
The Everlasting works its will.
The slayer and the slain may be
Knit in a secret harmony.
What does the spirit urge us to ?
Some sacrifice that may undo
The bonds that hold us to the clay,
And limit life to this cold day ?
Some for a gentle dream will die :
Some for an empire's majesty :
Some for a loftier humankind,
Some to be free as cloud or wind,

Will leave their valley, climb their slope.
Whate'er the deed, whate'er the hope,
Through all the varied battle cries
A Shepherd with a single voice
Still draws us nigh the Gates of Gold
That lead unto the heavenly fold.
So it may be that Michael died
For some far other countryside
Than that grey island he had known.
Yet on his dream of it was thrown
Some light from that consuming Fire
Which is the end of all desire.
If men adore It as the power,
Empires and cities, tower on tower,
Are built in worship by the way,
High Babylon or Nineveh.
Seek It as love and there may be
A Golden Age and Arcady.
All shadows are they of one thing
To which all life is journeying.

When he had made an end Rian said,
" Where, I wonder, in this universe of many
dimensions shall we really go after death ?
Is there one heavenly house for us all, or
will we live in ourselves as so many suppose,
our genius playing a fantasy on our memories
and desires ?   I remember one mystic telling
me that we all had a genie like Aladdin, and
it would build marvellous palaces for us and

exalt our dreams into unimaginable light. Such solitary magnificence would please Leroy more than me. I am a sociable person, but I am now too drowsy for more speculation." Leroy, as tireless in mind as Lavelle, would have made a commentary on all that had been said, but he saw Lavelle was sinking into reverie and was not inclined for further speech, so he made a pretence of imitating Rian, who was trying to sleep in a chair. But no sleep during the night came to that restless soul.

XX

FROM the recess of the window Lavelle gazed into the night enveloping the monstrous fabric of the city. In an abeyance of will brought about by weariness he became oppressed by the melancholy which so often arises through contemplation of an external vastness in which humanity becomes dwarfed, and what seemed lofty in the heart shrivels to littleness by the measurement of the eye. Beyond the murky city shining seas were rolling by shadowy mountains, and over them heavens which lost themselves in their own depths, rumouring their own infinitudes, fainting and faltering in their speech, for light, though it be swiftest of all things, ere it has found a final resting-place or hamlet in the gloom, the worlds it spake of have long ceased to be. The stare of the night seemed pitiless and immutable, and he did not then remember that those heavens had always echoed his mood and were gay or

174

solemn as he was exultant or mournful,
reflecting as a glass from hour to hour the
transformations in his own spirit. The
poetic nature has all childhood's excess of
emotion, and in an anguish such as the heart
of childhood might hold he thought of the
Golden Age passed away from the world
and the terrible and material powers ruling
in the Iron Age. Through a night of
time endless to his imagination he foresaw
the martyrdom of those who like himself
had nourished longing for the light and an
earth made gay by a laughter which was
worse than sobbing. Out of this meditation
arose an immense pity for life ; and because
the sadness was spiritual and was not for
himself, was indeed self-forgetful, it was
marvellously rolled away and a deep serenity
took its place. He felt the universe was
sweet at heart, and that same majesty which
had played with him as a boy among the
hills was with him and he knew it would be
with him to the end, and by it all dreams
would be fulfilled. He murmured to himself the words of promise " Long lost hearts
burn in the oil of the lamp of the King."
Like a spell the utterance quickened a
memory which had kept his life austere for

many years, and a young beauty which had
been made dust glowed before him as if it
had never perished. She seemed to live in
a luminous and blessed air, and was running
to him along hills strangely like the hills
his boyhood knew, and face and eyes were
more ecstatic than life. " Oh, Magic !
Magic ! " he whispered, calling her by the
sweet name his fancy had bestowed on so
vivid and lovely a girlhood. Then form
and face faded, swallowed up in the Ever-
living out of which they came, and her last
look seemed to echo back the promise of
the words, " Long lost hearts burn in the
oil of the lamp of the King." And then his
yearning brought him nigh to the fountain
in which that and all other beauty had been
born ; and he knew that all that was cast
up by it was lovely, and if rust or decay came
over the spirit they were burned away as it
fell back into the fountain where it received
once more the primal blessings of youth,
ecstasy, and beauty. In that hour innumerable images of life, hopes, and dreams
hitherto uncomprehended, causes to which
he had closed his heart, men from whom he
had been remote in soul, all came nigh him
with some revelation of their inmost being

in which they reflected the ancient beauty.
In each was some ray of Eternal Mind. The
Eternal Mind going forth knew itself in
them, and they returning knew themselves
in it. The All-seeing and All-knowing had
not withheld life from any, and while they
were sustained by It and It had not con-
demned them, it was not for man to take life
away. He remembered the words of the
old man, " We should cast none out of the
heart." And brooding on himself he saw
how he had closed the doors to many by
devotion to one form of beauty only, and
he realised that what was cast out of the
heart must force entry by pain, for life would
be denied entry to none of its realms. All
this was revealed to him when thought had
ceased, and he was carried beyond himself,
and his spirit seemed to be bathed by some
shoreless ocean of sweet unterminable being.
Never was he so remote from the vision of
life, and never more intimate with being.
Everything was understood. Everything
was loved. Everything was forgiven. He
knew after that exaltation he could never
be the same again. Never could he be
fierce or passionate. And his wisdom must
be to retain this serenity, and he forbore to

think of the conflict that had brought him
there, and he stilled every earthly memory
lest he might be cast out from the spirit.
Through the night he sat with closed eyes
made radiant within and sustained by that
profundity of being men worship as the
Father. At last his eyes opened. A dawn
was beginning to lighten in the East. Gold
began to mix with the blue, and the armada
which had been floating invisibly in the high
air was fired by light from a sun not yet
over the horizon. He saw the old historian
seated beside him. His eyes were fixed on
Lavelle, and he whispered to the poet,
" You have come nigh to the Kingdom.
You have seen the Kingdom." Because of
that recognition Lavelle felt the old man
more the intimate of his spirit than even
that beauty he had so long remembered and
loved, but which had never shared with him
the revelation of the Eternal.

As the dawn kindled, the tumult in the
city, which had been stilled for a while, broke
out again furiously. There were shouts
and concussions and reverberations. The
prisoners in the great room woke from uneasy
slumbers. The conflict came closer to the
great building in which they were confined

and the rattle was deafening. Leroy, alert
as ever, was first to understand what was
taking place. " Our comrades are winning
in the city," he cried. " They are encircling
the arsenal."

He had hardly spoken when the door
opened and an officer appeared, who said,
" We may have to evacuate this building
and fight our way through the city. We
cannot take prisoners with us. I have to
tell you if we evacuate we shall blow up the
arsenal." The prisoners were silent for a
moment, but Leroy, always generous, said,
" This prisoner," pointing to Heyt, " is not
of us. He is here by error. He is for
empire and is not worthy to die with us."
He told the officer who Heyt was, and the
officer, startled by the name, sent for another,
who recognised the president of the Air
Federation. Lavelle would have intervened
on behalf of the old historian. But Brehon
placed his hand gently on the arm of the poet
and he knew it was forbidden. The
Imperialist, moved by what he had heard
and understanding these men were different
from all he had imagined of them, hesitated
for a moment as if he would have said or
urged something. Then he shook his head

as if he realised how impossible it now was to effect anything, and he left them without a word and went out to make the world in his own image.

THE END

Printed in Great Britain by R. & R. CLARK, LIMITED, *Edinburgh.*

www.ingramcontent.com/pod-product-compliance
Lightning Source LLC
Chambersburg PA
CBHW021059090426

42738CB00006B/415